Shakespeare's
THE
SONNETS

UNICIO J. VIOLI
ASSOCIATE PROFESSOR OF ENGLISH
FAIRLEIGH DICKINSON UNIVERSITY

**MONARCH
PRESS**

CONTENTS

SHAKESPEARE'S LIFE: A BRIEF SURVEY

SHAKESPEARE'S LIFE. We celebrate Shakespeare's birthday on the twenty-third of April because a great English holiday occurs on that day, St. George's Day. St. George is the patron saint of England, and it is fitting that we celebrate his birthday then. We have no record of his birthdate, but we do know that he was christened William Shakespeare on April twenty-sixth in the year of our lord, 1564. His father was a glover and a seller of timber, wool, etc. His mother was of good family who brought her husband some wealth in land and gentility.

STRATFORD is a town (about a hundred miles northwest of London) which lies in the county of Warwickshire; it was a rich market center teeming with well-to-do burghers. Its grammar schools were free to sons of burgesses like John Shakespeare, Shakespeare's father. Shakespeare must have gone to such a school, where he would have been prepared for college by an intensive study of classical authors like Ovid and Cicero and by much training in grammar, logic, and rhetoric. The town was visited by touring companies which put on rather old-fashioned plays with stilted moral lessons as their prime end. Often the characters from such plays were taken directly from the Bible or given allegorical names such as Vice, Good-Deeds, Good-Angel, Bad-Angel, Lechery, Hypocrisy, Providence, Grace, etc. It follows that as a boy Shakespeare must have seen many of these morality plays and been influenced by them. Note, for example, the morality-like quality of *Measure for Measure,* even to the naming of characters; we have Mistress Overdone, Angelo (angel), Vincentio (conquerer), Lucio (lust), etc. Shakespeare obtained from Stratford a love of countryside flowers, animals, sports, and above all local characters such as petty constables, priests, schoolmasters, tradesmen, and many other middle-class types. Our next record tells us that in 1582 William married an Ann Hathaway, a relatively poor farmer's daughter; she was twenty-three and he eighteen. Susan, their first child, was born six months later. One good theory is that Shakespeare and Ann were engaged through public announcement; that is "betrothed," which would have made pregnancy legitimate even before marriage, providing marriage followed. Twins, Hamnet and Judith, were born in 1585, and not long after that William left for London, leaving his family in Stratford. From then he stayed on in London, but continued to support his family, visited them, perhaps frequently, bought extensive properties in Stratford-Upon-Avon, secured his father a gentleman's coat of arms, and in

5

his later years returned to Stratford. In 1616 at the age of fifty-two he died rich, leaving much property.

LONDON. William was about twenty-two (1586) when he arrived in London. He very likely joined up with The Lord Chamberlain's Men in 1594, after having served several years of apprenticeship in the theater. He was actor, manager, playwright, and stockholder during his career in the theater, which ran for the rest of his life until retirement. His career can be divided into four main parts (according to the critic and authority Peter Alexander and others).

EARLY COMEDIES AND HISTORIES. Here in London he learned his trade, adapting Latin classical comedy (*Comedy of Errors*), Italian romantic comedy (*Two Gentlemen of Verona*), Italian rip-roaring farce (*Taming of the Shrew*), bloody sensational melo-drama (*Titus Andronicus*), and popular plays on English history glorifying the past so as to give honor to his Tudor queen, Elizabeth. The history plays teach good civic lessons such as the evils of civil strife, the mob-like sheepheadedness of the lower classes under evil, the villainy of machiavellian demagogues, and the great virtues of patriotism, courage on the field of battle, and above all the sacredness of kingship and its rights, duties, and privileges. Examples are the three parts of *Henry VI, Richard III, King John.* During 1592-4 when the plague closed all theaters, the ever-busy William wrote some superb and lively (if erotic) poems (*Venus and Adonis, Rape of Lucrece,* and many of the sonnets) which appealed to the Elizabethan upper classes especially. By 1594 he had already shown his prowess in the theater, even though much of his playwriting was imitative and rather poor in quality.

GROWING MATURITY: 1594-1599. This is the time of his greatest popularity, a period in which his plays seem to reflect gaiety, romance, and the highest optimism. Plays like the two parts of *Henry IV, The Merchant of Venice, A Midsummer Night's Dream, The Merry Wives of Windsor, As You Like It,* and *Twelfth Night* are charming, witty, exciting, breathless in their pace, master-pieces in their own right. Even his tragedy *Romeo and Juliet* is ro-mantic, the final fate of the lovers a product of fate and not character. In these plays his art of characterization is at its height. Immortals like Falstaff, Shylock, Puck Bottom, Jacques Touchstone Rosalind, Sir Toby Belch, Sir Andrew and Malvolio crowd the stage. These characters were taken from life: the countryside, the throng-ing streets of London, the court. Even the plays laid in Italy, Vienna, France, and Greece reflect Elizabethan England!

THE MATURE PERIOD (GLOBE THEATER PERIOD: 1599-1608.)
In 1599 the Lord Chamberlain's Men obtained the great Globe
Theater, which was Shakespeare's major place of work for the
rest of his life. When Elizabeth died in 1603 the name of the company was changed to The King's Men. Needless to say, Shakespeare's company was the rage of London, its popularity overwhelm-
ing. Royal sponsorship and favor were never lacking. A cross section
of the London populace attended his plays avidly; however, about
the time of King James, the middle classes dropped off in attend-
ance, and upper classes began to form more and more a larger
proportion of the audience. In these nine years we have such great
masterpieces as *Hamlet, Othello, King Lear, Macbeth, Antony
and Cleopatra;* and lesser masterpieces like *Julius Caesar, All's
Well That Ends Well, Measure for Measure,* and *Coriolanus.*

RECONCILIATION AND PEACE: 1608-1616. In 1608 an upper
class indoor theater called Blackfriars Theatre was purchased by
Shakespeare's company. For such an audience he wrote *Pericles,
Cymbeline, The Winter's Tale, The Tempest, and Henry VIII.*
Filled with allegory of great subtlety combined with fantastically
unrealistic plots and idealized characters, they appeal to people
of refined and intellectual taste. His idealism, his spirit of forgiveness, his compassionate love for mankind take on an almost
mystical quality. The poetry is refined, highly subtle and exquisite.

INTRODUCTION

COMMENTARY AND EDITIONS: Next to *Hamlet*, the Shakespearean work which has given rise to more commentary and stirred up more controversy than any of his other works is the *Sonnets*, first published in 1609. The reason for much of this voluminous commentary lies in the fact that we do not know when they were written or to whom, if written to anyone at all. We do not even know whether they reveal an autobiographical story, as is claimed. Wordsworth believed that Shakespeare unlocked his heart in the *Sonnets*, but Browning concluded that, if this were so ". . . the less Shakespeare he!"

The *Sonnets* first appeared in print in 1609 when Shakespeare was forty-five years old. The title page of this first edition reads: "SHAKE-SPEARES SONNETS Never before imprinted. At London By G. Eld for T. T. and are to be sold by *John Wright*, dwelling at Christ Church gate. 1609." (This means that the book was printed in London by G. Eld at the request of the editor of the sonnets, Thomas Thorpe, the "T. T." of the title page, and that the *Sonnets* were to be sold at John Wright's bookshop, situated at the gate of Christ Church.) Most scholars think that Thorpe published the poems without Shakespeare's permission in view of the many errors and misprints in this original Quarto edition. Modern editors have, however, corrected these errors, though largely on the basis of educated guesswork, called "emendations."

The best of the modern scholars are Craig, Alexander, Dover-Wilson, Hubler and, especially, Hyder Rollins, who edited the important *Variorum* edition. In the *Variorum*, we find the original text of the 1609 Quarto edition along with commentary on the poems and text compiled from the writings of a great many scholars and critics. The extensive discussions of all the major issues and problems make this easily the most valuable single volume for anyone seriously interested in a study of the sonnets.

ARRANGEMENT OF SONNETS: Although most scholars do not accept Thorpe's ordering of the *Sonnets*, it is still most convenient to use his numbering, especially as no other arrangement has any independent authority. Following Thorpe's numbering, then, the 154 sonnets would seem to fall into two main groups. The first major grouping, numbers 1-126, seem to be addressed to a handsome youth, or at least such a young man is the subject of these poems. Within this larger group, there are two special sub-sections, numbers 1-17, which exhort the youth to marry and have children to insure his immortality, and numbers 78-86, which deal with a "Rival Poet" who temporarily wins the favor and, presumably, patronage, of the friend. The second major grouping, numbers 127-152, are addressed to a "Dark Lady," or at least such a dark-haired woman is the subject of these poems. This "Dark Lady" is the mistress of the poet and, for a period, of the friend as well. The two final sonnets, numbers 153 and 154, are unrelated to the previous sequence, being free translations of a fifth century A. D. Greek poem about Cupid and his torch.

THE FRIEND: The identity of the youth addressed in sonnets 1-126 is unknown though scholars have suggested certain candidates. Some say the young man was William Herbert (Third Earl of Pembroke), some say Henry Wriothesley (Third Earl of Southampton), but there are many other lesser candidates such as William Harte (Shakespeare's nephew), Willie Hughes (Oscar Wilde's pet theory), William Hathaway, William Hall, William Harvey, and even William Himself! As can be seen, all of the candidates have the initials W. H. (or in the case of Southampton, H. W.), for these initials are the only evidence we have regarding the friend's identification.

The source of this evidence is the 1609 edition. On the back of the title page of this original edition, there is the following dedication:

TO THE ONLIE BEGETTER OF
THESE INSVING SONNETS
Mr W. H. ALL HAPPINESSE
AND THAT ETERNITIE
PROMISED
BY
OUR EVER-LIVING POET
WISHETH
THE WELL-WISHING
ADVENTURER IN
SETTING
FORTH

Since the editor, Thomas Thorpe, calls Mr. W. H. the "onlie begetter" of these sonnets, it might appear that someone with the initials W. H. obtained the manuscript of the *Sonnets* for Thorpe to publish. But most scholars believe that the phrase "onlie begetter" means, rather, the person who was the subject of the sonnets and their inspirer since Thorpe refers to "that eternitie promised by our ever-living poet" to W. H. and this promise of poetic immortality is the subject of many of the sonnets addressed to the friend from sonnet 18 on through the first major grouping of the sonnets.

The primary candidate is Henry Wriothesley, Third Earl of Southampton, who was twenty in 1593, the year in which many of the sonnets to the youth were probably written. As Shakespeare had dedicated his two erotic narrative poems, *Venus and Adonis* (1593) and *The Rape of Lucrece* (1594), to Southampton, and as the dedication to *Lucrece* was couched in language suggesting their close acquaintance, the Southampton theory would seem to have some weight, even though his initials are the reverse of those in the dedication to the *Sonnets*.

To those who consider the reversal of Southampton's initials to be a serious detraction from his candidacy, the qualifications of William Herbert, Third Earl of Pembroke, seem more appropriate. Like Southampton, Pembroke was an extremely wealthy aristocrat, a great patron of poets and other writers, and a most sensual man who despised the institution of marriage. Both Earls were handsome and stylish youths at the time Shakespeare was presumably writing his sonnets. Pembroke, however, was only thirteen in 1593, the year in which many scholars would date some of the sonnets, and the exhortation for such a young boy to marry would appear to be ridiculous. For the Pembroke theory to fit, then, the sonnets would have to be dated at about 1600.

THE QUESTION OF HOMOSEXUALITY: Although this first group of sonnets address a male youth in the most endearing terms, Shakespeare does not appear to have been a homosexual. On this point the best scholars are agreed. And the sonnets themselves provide the best proof of this. Sonnet 20 openly declares that Shakespeare is interested only in the young man's spiritual love. He clearly states that the youth's sexual parts are dedicated exclusively to the ladies. On the other hand, Shakespeare's own sexual love, constantly mentioned in the "Dark Lady" sonnets (127-152), is as clearly directed towards a woman. In fact, his sexual lust for her is positively frightening in its compulsive deterioration of his character, a psychological fact which finally drives him into religious despair (in the important religious sonnet 146). The first 126 sonnets may address the youth in the most endearing terms, but the love is always clearly Platonic in the popular sense of the word and generally in its philosophic sense as well. In Platonic terms (See Plato's *Symposium*), love is compared to a ladder with many rungs, the highest of which is devoid of sex and entirely spiritual, the whole process of rising on the ladder of love being a process in which the lovers are primarily concerned with their own spiritual betterment and in aiding that of the beloved. In this regard, Shakespeare claims to be inspired to his best poetic efforts by his friend, often guiding his friend toward spiritual improvement in almost pedagogical terms. Such Platonic love between male friends was considered by many in the Renaissance to be the highest form of love possible on earth. In many of Shakespeare's plays, male friendships are treated in such exalted terms, the friendship of Hamlet and Horatio being the most obvious example. In addition, the Renaissance mode in writing letters or dedications, which continued well into the eighteenth century, was to use the language of devoted love. Thus amorous terms, when used between male friends, carried no necessarily questionable content.

THEMES INVOLVING THE FRIEND: Shakespeare's approach to his beloved friend is marked by three main themes. The first seventeen sonnets exhort the youth to marry and beget children. One of Shakespeare's major arguments in this regard is drawn from the Biblical "Parable of the Talents" (*Matthew* 25: 14-30). In Jesus' parable, a lord, going on a journey, gave his three servants various amounts of "talents" (an ancient Roman coin) depending upon their abilities. Two of them invested their sums profitably while the third, who had received only one talent, buried his in the ground. Upon returning, the lord demanded an accounting of what his servants had done with the money he had lent them. He was so satisfied by the investments of his first two servants that he promoted them to more responsible tasks, but he was angry with the servant who buried his talent, and took this one talent away from him, saying: "For unto every one that hath shall be given, and he shall have abundance: but from him that hath not shall be taken away even that which he hath" (*Matt.* 25: 29). The generally accepted interpretation of this parable is that God has given certain rich gifts or abilities to man which are to be put to use, not hoarded, such hoarding being against the law of God. In the application of this parable to his friend, Shakespeare argues that his friend is hoarding God's gift of beauty (sometimes termed "Nature's" gift) by not producing children who would preserve his beauty for future generations, and so his beauty will eventually be taken from him. A second Biblical parable is also alluded to, although less importantly, and this is the "Parable of the Prodigal Son" (*Luke* 15: 11-32). In this parable of Jesus, a man has two sons, one dutiful and the other a rioter. After many years of waste and delinquency, the rioter returns home penitent and is immediately forgiven. In fact, he is feted more extravagantly than the dutiful son ever has been. The reason for this is that "joy shall be in heaven over one sinner that repenteth more than over ninety and nine just persons, which need no repentance." (*Lk*. 15: 7). In applying this parable, Shakespeare argues again that his friend is wasting his heritage but may be redeemed and receive manifold rewards by repentance. In these arguments, Shakespeare is playing the role of Platonic pedagogue to his beloved young friend.

Beginning with Sonnet 18, and continuing here and there throughout the first major grouping of sonnets, Shakespeare approaches the problem of mutability and the effects of time upon his beloved friend in a different fashion. Though time and death work together to rob man, and particularly the friend, of his youth and beauty putting ugly wrinkles in his face and finally causing his death, the friend's beauty can be made immortal in spite of the ravages of time and death. Shakespeare asserts that his poetry will survive the destructive effects and, since the subject of this poetry is his friend's beauty it will immortalize his beloved friend's beauty. In a third related group of sonnets, however, Shakespeare does not treat his friend's beauty as subject to decay but as the perfect model of beauty of which the many other beauties on earth are but expressions. This is a classic Platonic concept as modified by neo-platonic thought.

THE DARK LADY: After 126 sonnets to his young male friend, Shakespeare begins, in Sonnet 127, to write directly to and of a "Dark Lady." No one knows who this dark-skinned, dark-eyed and dark-haired lady could have been in spite of the mass of guesswork which has been written in an attempt to establish her identity; but she was, at all events, the evil angel who tempted Shakespeare to commit sins of the flesh and who tormented him with her infidelities. In her most devilish infidelity, she lures his young friend from his side; the two male friends caught in the toils of a provocative slut (for that is the way in which Shakespeare describes her, and worse). To crown his cup of misery, the youth finally betrays their friendship completely by stealing Shakespeare's mistress away from him. This double betrayal by both his spiritual and sexual loves is the most anguishing event in the sonnets, and produces some of his most tragic and tortured verses, some of which also appear, without full explanation, in the earlier group of sonnets addressed to the friend.

The Dark Lady sonnets also contain many sexual allusions, most of them concealed in the form of puns, without an understanding of which there would be little understanding of these sonnets at all. For, though Shakespeare was tormented by his compulsive lust for a promiscuous and cruel female, he was still capable of treating his problem and the whole situation with wit, as, indeed, he does with many a subject in the whole sonnet sequence. The poetic habit of the day was to display one's wit through clever handling of language, the ability to find appropriate puns, similes, metaphors and extended conceits, and also through apparently paradoxical turns of thought. The chief proponents of this type of poetic wit were a group of seventeenth century poets, later termed "Metaphysical," whose chief practitioners were Donne, Herbert, Vaughan and Crashaw. But the greatest and wittiest of them all was Shakespeare, himself, the Dark Lady sonnets being a particular gold mine of such wit, especially with regard to sexual word play, a form of wit which also appears extensively throughout Shakespeare's plays.

THE RIVAL POET: The third important character in the action of the sonnets is the so-called "Rival Poet" who appears importantly in Sonnets 78-86. This Rival Poet curries the favor of Shakespeare's youthful friend and patron and apparently wins it, at least temporarily, an episode which also affords Shakespeare a good deal of pain. George Chapman is the favorite candidate for the role of Rival Poet although we have no evidence to show that either Southampton or Pembroke was ever his patron. Other candidates are Daniel, Drayton, Barnes, Marlowe and Markham. All we know of the Rival Poet from the sonnets is that Shakespeare considered him to be learned, presumably a university graduate, which Shakespeare was not.

HISTORY AND FORMS OF THE SONNET: The Italian poets were the first to write in the sonnet form. Their greatest genius in this form was Francesco Petrarco, known in English as Petrarch, who lived from 1304 to 1374. At the age of thirteen, Petrarch first saw the girl named Laura who was to inspire his odes and sonnets, poems for which, in 1341, he was crowned Poet Laureate at Rome. Although he was one of the greatest of Renaissance humanists, a rediscoverer of the pagan world, and a lover of learning, his most important achievement for us was his fixing of the form of the sonnet, a poetic form which enjoyed an enormous vogue throughout Europe, spreading through France to England. In the 1590's, when Shakespeare began writing his sonnets, the vogue of the Petrarch sonnet was at its highest, Sir Philip Sidney, Spenser, Drayton, Daniel, Wyatt and Surrey all having written importantly in this form. It was of that form that Ben Jonson, Shakespeare's learned contemporary, once said that he "cursed Petrarch for redacting verses to Sonnets; which he said were like that Tirrants bed, wher some who were too short were racked, others too long cut short" (as reported to Drummond and published in 1619).

Most poets, however, have found the sonnet form attractive precisely because of its demands.

The Petrarchan sonnet form demands the following discipline:

1. *Length:* A sonnet must contain exactly fourteen lines within which a single theme is to be developed in accordance with a rigid format.

2. *Rhyme scheme*: The Petrarchan *rhyme scheme* is either *abba abba abba cde cde,* or *abba abba edc edc,* or finally, *abba abba dec dec;* in any case, the first eight lines are arranged in two groups of four lines each, these four lines being known as a *quatrain,* these two *quatrains* together being known as an *octave.* The final six lines, in which the variations in rhyming pattern occur, are known as the *sestet.* As the Petrarchan sonnet employs only five different rhymes (abcde), this rhyming pattern requires immense linguistic resources in like-rhymes.

3. *Structure*: There are two parts to the sonnet, the *octave,* in which the "problem" is stated and developed, and the *sestet,* in which the problem is "resolved", a resolution which generally involves a turn of thought. Sometimes this pure form is modified so that the *octave* acts as two separate *quatrains* in which the problem is repeated twice in two different images.

Whether or not it was because the English language is not as rich in rhymes as the Italian, a modified form of the sonnet rose in England known as the Elizabethan or Shakespearean sonnet, although it was Sir Thomas Wyatt and the Earl of Surrey rather than Shakespeare who invented the English variation. Bringing the sonnet form from Italy to England, they developed a rhyme scheme which was perhaps more suitable to the English language. This rhyming pattern is as follows: *abab cdcd efef gg.* As opposed to the Petrarchan rhyme scheme which uses only five different rhymes, the English sonnet uses eight different rhymes, the final rhyme appearing in the last two lines which therefore become what is known as a *couplet.* This change in rhyme scheme completely alters the nature of the sonnet form, particularly in the division of *octave* and *sestet.* As opposed to the interlinked rhyming of the Petrarchan *octave* (*abba abba*) which makes it into essentially a single unit, the rhyming of the first eight lines of the Shakespearean sonnet (*abab cdcd*) produce what is more properly considered two separate quatrains. And the same is true of the remaining six lines. Whereas the Petrarchan *octave* actually contains within it three *couplets,* not counting the first and last lines (*bb aa bb*).

the Petrarchan *sestet,* with its three repeated rhymes, avoids all possibility of a *couplet* thus producing a more unified section. The last six lines of the Shakespearean sonnet, however, easily break into a third *quatrain* with concluding *couplet.* Now, although the Shakespearean sonnet sometimes functions like a Petrarchan sonnet, the first eight lines stating the problem and the last six resolving it, the function of the Petrarchan *octave* is all too often given to all three *quatrains,* which state the problem in three different ways, leaving only the *couplet* to resolve the problem, often taking the form of a neat aphorism. The Shakespearean sonnet form is, then, essentially less subtle and less tightly woven than the Petrarchan form and, although some English sonneteers continued to use the Petrarchan form, most notably Spenser and, later, Milton, most did not, and among these was the greatest of all English sonneteers, Shakespeare.

SUBJECT MATTER OF SONNETS: Although the form of the sonnet was developed by Petrarch, its subject matter dealt with a style of love which had been developed two centuries earlier by the troubadours of Southern France. In the conventions of this love, known as "courtly love," the lady is worshipped as if she were the Virgin Mary, the vocabulary of Christianity being converted to the lady's worship. She is divine, holy, and the ideal of beauty: white-skinned, rosy-cheeked, lily-handed, blonde—and she constantly rejects her adoring lover. The haughty indifference of the supremely beautiful lady-love leaves her woebegone lover sighing, complaining, weeping, pleading and wailing fruitlessly. The two hardly touch each other except, perhaps, for a consolatory kiss.

Along with such other anti-Petrarchan poets as John Donne, however, Shakespeare pulls Petrarch's blonde ideal from her pedestal and turns her into a sly, dark wench. On the other hand, he made his friend, with some qualifications, into a kind of male model of the Petrarchan female ideal, unusual as well in the sonnet literature. For, although the youth seems almost feminine in his appearance from Shakespeare's descriptions—certainly not our ideal of masculine attractiveness—Shakespeare addresses him as the ideal of beauty, the perfect creation of Nature, Nature's darling, beauty itself! But perhaps most important of all is the differing form of love conveyed in these sonnets, particularly with regard to the relationship of Shakespeare and the friend. Although we had earlier stressed the Platonic, spiritual quality of their love, its less ideal characteristics are perhaps even more important. The story of their love, as far as we can call it a story, describes in great detail and with great scrupulosity the mutual infidelities of the poet and friend, infidelities which lead to bitter recriminations and shame and finally to a mature reconciliation and deepened love. It is a flawed love, very like that of Shakespeare's Antony and Cleopatra, understood and accepted in the pitiless rush of time, which is one of the chief glories of Shakespeare's immortal *Sonnets*.

(1)—"from fairest creatures..."

SUMMARY: *Beauty that does not reproduce itself by producing offspring is both cruel and wasteful. Take pity on the world or else be regarded by it as selfish.*

PARAPHRASE

1. We desire offspring from the fairest of creatures
2. so that beauty's perfection ["rose"] may never disappear;
3. but as beauty does age and die off in good time,
4. its young heirs might continue to preserve their parents' memory.
5. But you are engaged to be wedded only to your bright eyes
6. and to go on feeding that love with fuel from your own body,
7. making a famine where abundance lies:
8. you are your own foe, too cruel to your own sweet self.
9. You, who are now the world's fresh flower,
10. a harbinger of the lovely spring,
11. are burying your sperm-seed within your own testicle (bud);
12. and in this way, beloved miser, you squander your potential fatherhood by selfishly hoarding it within your own body.
13.   Take pity on the world, or else keep on being selfish—
14.   by consuming in yourself what is owed to the world and death.

COMMENT: This is the first of 126 sonnets addressed to a young man, extremely lovely in face and figure, the very epitome of beauty. Numbers 1-17 appeal to Shakespeare's young friend to have children so that his beauty will endure in his offspring. Nature in her *plenitude* (God's plenty) does not place her gifts without requiring an equal obligation on the part of the recipient.

(2)—"when forty winters..."

SUMMARY: *Since your beauty will have disappeared by the time you reach forty, it behooves you to preserve it by recreating it in offspring.*

PARAPHRASE

1. When you are forty years [winters] old,
2. with deep wrinkles on your beautiful features,
3. your youthful outward appearance [livery], so admired by all now,
4. will be turned to a ragged garment [weed] of little value.
5. Then, if you are asked, "where is that former beauty?
6. Where is that loveliness [treasure] of your vigorous youth?";
7. to reply that it remains still in your deeply sunken eyes
8. were an all-consuming shame and useless praise.
9. How much more praise you would deserve if your beauty were put to use, and
10. if you could answer: "This beautiful child of mine
11. shall pay in full my debt to Nature and be the excuse for my old age."
12. thus, your beauty will be inherited and preserved in your child.
13.   In this way you will be re-created in your old age,
14.   and you will see your own blood flowing warm in him when you feel your own to be cold.

COMMENT: Notice Shakespeare's fondness for envisaging the most profound and abstruse thoughts as vivid pictures or images: Winter is pictured as a besieging army entrenched around a field of beauty. Youth is pictured as "proud livery" and a "treasure" (Note: *lusty, deep-sunken, sum my count* all refer to treasure).

(3)—"look in thy glass..."

SUMMARY: *You will re-create your beauty by marrying and begetting offspring, but if you die single, your beauty also perishes.*

PARAPHRASE

1. Look in your mirror and tell the face you see that
2. now is the time you should have a child to preserve that image;
3. if you do not renew your face's healthful condition,
4. you cheat the world, and leave some potential mother unblessed.
5. For where is the woman so beautiful, whose
6. untouched [uneared] womb
7. would spurn your sexual fertilization [tillage]?
8. Or who is he so foolish as to make a tomb of his body, and by self-love put an end to posterity?
9. You are the mirror-image of your mother, and she in you

10. recalls the lovely period of her youth.
11. So your own old eyes will see,
12. despite your wrinkles, this lovely period of your youth.
13.   But if you live unremembered in children and
14.   die single, your image then perishes with you.

> **COMMENT:** Shakespeare, like many in his time, was fond of
> sexual terms couched in farmers' imagery: a virgin has an
> *uneared* womb; *husbandry* (homemaking) involves *tillage* or
> plowing of the land (*uneared*=unploughed; *tillage*=plow-
> ing=sexual act). The youth is evidently the image of a very
> lovely mother. Although this was especially true of the Earl
> of Southampton's mother, Herbert's mother was also lovely
> and said to resemble her son.

(4)—"unthrifty loveliness..."

SUMMARY: *You refuse to return Nature's loan of beauty, and
consequently it will perish with you unless preserved in offspring.*

PARAPHRASE

1. Unprofitable beauty, why do you spend
2. upon yourself the legacy of beauty that you have inherited?
3. Nature gives nothing outright but merely lends,
4. and, being generous, she makes loans only to those who are
   generous.
5. Then, beautiful miser, why do you abuse
6. her bounteous gift lent you to pass on?
7. Unprofitable trader, why do you employ
8. so great a gift of beauty, and yet are unable to preserve it?
9. For, trading in your beauty with yourself alone,
10. you merely cheat your own sweet self.
11. Then how, when Nature calls for you to die,
12. can you leave behind an acceptable account of yourself?
13.   Your unused beauty will then be buried with you,
14.   which, if put to use, would live on in your children as
       executors of that beauty.

> **COMMENT:** The *conceit* (clever image of comparison) per-
> vading this sonnet is taken from the business field: Nature is
> looked upon as one who leaves a *legacy* (beauty) which is to
> be put to *profitable use* (a word meaning both the employment
> of money profitably and the act of sexual intercourse). Note

such words as *miser, abuse, gift, trading, cheat, niggard, bounteous, largesse, profitless, usurer* (one who lends money at interest), *sum of sums, traffic* (which in Shakespeare's day could mean money-exchange). An especially admirable—and clever—conceit is that in 11-12, where Nature is compared to Death calling for an accounting (audit) of her legacy of beauty. This recalls the parable of the Prodigal Son (Luke 15:11-32),—a motif strongly recurrent in the sonnets in which a wastrel son, after a life of riot, returns to his father, penitent, and is immediately forgiven.

(5)—"those hours . . ."

SUMMARY: *Beautiful and lovely summer inevitably leads on to bare winter; and if there is no preservation of summer's essence, there is left no memory of summer's beauty. Your beauty, like that of a flower's essence, can be preserved in children.*

PARAPHRASE

1. Time, who gently shaped
2. your lovely beauty, the focus of all men's eyes,
3. will prove merciless to that very same beauty,
4. and make ugly that which surpasses all in beauty.
5. For never-resting Time leads summer on
6. to hideous winter, at which time summer's beauty is destroyed;
7. summer's sap is frozen in frost, leaves fall,
8. beauty is covered with snow and there is bareness everywhere.
9. Then, if summer's essence were not preserved and distilled,
10. like perfume imprisoned in a vial,
11. both the beauty and its essence would be lost,
12. leaving no trace of what its beauty was like.
13. But if flowers are distilled into perfume, even though they die,
14. they lose but their shape; their essence sweetly endures.

COMMENT: The conceit here is the comparison of the friend and his posterity with summer's beauty and the perfume of its flowers distilled into a small glass. If Shakespeare's beautiful friend does not preserve the essence of his beauty by producing children, as perfume preserves the essence of summer flowers, it will die with him. The metaphor is still more vivid when we realize that the Elizabethan fancier of poetry would have visualized testicular (9-14) containers filled with unused sperm as another extension of the conceit.

Other images: the hours (in line one a two-syllabic word pronounced "howers") as workmen fashioning the face of Shakespeare's friend; summer being led on by "never-resting time" to his doom and death.

Memorable lines:
"Beauty o'ersnow'd and bareness everywhere:" (1.8)
"A liquid prisoner pent in walls of glass." (1.10)

(6)—"then let not winter's . . ."

SUMMARY: *Your essence of beauty preserved in children will defeat death itself.*

PARAPHRASE

1. Then do not let Time [winter] deface
2. your youth [summer] before you can leave behind the essence of beauty;
3. preserve your sweet beauty in a vial (child?); make rich some place
4. with the treasure of your beauty, before it is destroyed with you.
5. That charging of interest is not forbidden usury
6. which makes those happy to pay the interest to which they have agreed most willingly;
7. therefore, it is up to you to create another like yourself,
8. or—that which is ten times better—ten more like you.
9. Ten offspring like yourself are better than you alone are,
10. if that ten multiplied your beauteous image by ten more;
11. then what could death do, if you were to die, since you would
12. be preserved in your posterity?
13.   Do not be stubborn: you are much too fair
14.   to be conquered by Death, leaving your beauty for worms to inherit.

COMMENT: This sonnet continues the message and conceit of Sonnet 5: the perfume sperm) must be preserved in pregnating via his sperm some woman (the vial). 2. by distilling the perfume of sweet flowers in a glass.

Other images: beauty is compared to a treasure (4); the lover is pictured as repaying a willing loan (6) to a happy recipient i.e., the lady). Since ten per cent was the highest rate of interest allowed under Queen Elizabeth, one grasps immediately the clever play upon that number (8-10).

(7)—"lo, in the orient . . ."

SUMMARY: *Unless you beget a son you will be admired by men only as long as you remain at the height of your beauty; for when age comes upon you, that admiration will disappear.*

PARAPHRASE

1. Behold, in the east when the lovely light
2. of the sun appears, each person on earth
3. pays homage to the new sunlight,
4. humbly greeting the sun as a sacred king;
5. and after having climbed up steeply in the sky,
6. like a strong youth in his prime,
7. mortals on earth worship its beauty still,
8. following attentively the sun's golden progress.
9. But when the sun, having reached its very zenith,
10. sinks down in the sky [the west] like a feeble old man,
11. men's eyes, formerly dutiful, now glance
12. away from its low path in the sky.
13.   So you, passing beyond your zenith of beauty
14.   will die unremembered—unless you have a son.

COMMENT: This sonnet takes much from classical sources, especially in the sun metaphor, for the sun is pictured as the driver of a chariot (*car*) pulled by fiery horses, which is the standard classical image: the sun god Apollo driving his fiery chariot across the sky—the *golden pilgrimage.* Here the sun is compared to Shakespeare's beloved friend: at its very height in the sky the sun is most dazzling; so too the friend is at his best in the period of youth (prime). Attendant associations are those of royalty, as in such words as *gracious, majesty,* the *homage* paid the sun by "each under eye" (mankind); the royalty symbols here, say some critics, imply nobility and blue blood in Shakespeare's friend. There is no doubt that this is often implied in the sonnets.

(8)—"music to hear . . ."

SUMMARY: *Just as music when played in chordal harmony is much better than a single part, so you will sound a most pleasant harmony with wife and child.*

PARAPHRASE

1. You whose voice is music to hear, why are you saddened at the sound of music?
2. Sweet does not conflict with sweet; joy delights in joy:
3. Why do you love music which does not gladden you,
4. or else receive with pleasure that which does you harm?
5. If the harmony of well-tuned sounds
6. in musical chords offends your ear,
7. it is merely reproaching you for preventing yourself, by your
8. bachelorhood, from becoming a husband and father of children [bearer of parts].
9. Note how one string, sweetly paired with another,
10. makes a chord of mutual harmony—
11. just like a father and child and happy mother,
12. who sing one pleasant note in unison.
13. Their harmony, being separate strains, seems as one note,
14. singing this refrain to you: "If you remain single, you shall end up as nothing."

COMMENT: Man-made music was an earthly manifestation of the heavenly strains made by the planets revolving in their spheres and heard only by angels. It was believed that the harmony of heaven could be discerned by the soul when man listened to earthly music. It was the yearning of the soul for the higher kind of music which made men sad. The speaker of the poem (Shakespeare) argues, however, that his friend is being reproached for disrupting the harmony of nature, which God ordained for man, by refusing to marry and procreate.

Because of its association with the *music of the spheres,* earthly music was held in high regard among Elizabethans. Most educated Elizabethans were more or less proficient in music; if one attended a party, he was often expected to sing or play in harmony with others by sight-reading the music part. The lute, with all except one of its strings in pairs (like the mandolin today), was an extremely popular instrument of the day. If one of the paired strings was struck, its mate sounded out without being struck, in what is known as "sympathetic harmony." Here the conceit is the harmony of lute music as compared to domestic harmony—man, wife, children.

(9)—"is it for fear..."

SUMMARY: *If beauty is not put to use (by having offspring), it* *destroys both beauty itself and the possessor of it. Such a crime against self and beauty is like a shameful murder.*

PARAPHRASE

1. Is it for fear of leaving an unhappy widow grieving for you
2. that you spend your life in bachlorhood?
3. Ah, but if you should die childless,
4. the world will mourn you like an unmated wife;
5. the world will lament you (as a widow her husband), weeping
6. that you did not leave a child behind,
7. since each widow retains clearly
8. in her mind her husband's shape as seen through their children.
9. Whatever the spendthrift squanders in the world
10. is but given to someone else, and the world will always enjoy it;
11. but the squandering of beauty ends in a dead end;
12. for, if not put to use, the beauty is destroyed along with its possessor.
13. No love for others can be found in the breast
14. of one who commits such a shameful murder upon himself.

COMMENT: Here the image is that of a widow compared to the world: as the widow weeps for a lost husband, so will the world weep for the lost beauty you have carried away with you. Note that the metaphor is not strictly logical since a widow's status and the friend's are not quite the same. Note the use of the Prodigal Son motif in *unthrift* (see Introduction for reference and explanation of the entire parable); The world of commerce intrudes again in such words as *unthrift* (9), *waste* (12), *user* and *unus'd* (12), the last two also carrying sexual meanings.

(10)—"for shame..."

SUMMARY: *You must hate yourself since without children you bring ruin upon both yourself and your family. Then for my sake, preserve your beauty in progeny.*

PARAPHRASE

1. For shame! how can you love others
2. when you are so selfish towards your own self?
3. Let it be granted, if you will, that you are loved by many,
4. still it is most evident that you love no one in return:
5. for you are so possessed by murderous hatred

6. that you do not even hesitate to conspire against yourself;
7. thus you seek to destroy your own family line,
8. where to continue it should be your chief desire.
9. O, change your mind, so that my opinion of you will also change!
10. Shall the feeling of hate be held by a person as beautiful as you, rather than the feeling of gentle love?
11. Be as your appearance really is, gracious and kind,
12. or at least be kind-hearted to your own self.
13.   Produce a child in your own likeness, out of love for me,
14.   so that beauty will endure in both you and in your offspring.

COMMENT: A common Renaissance ideal was that love is only known by its overt expression in life and humanity. Like a miser hoarding his money (a metaphor of which Shakespeare seems inordinately fond), love will wither away if not put to use: such behavior is unthrifty and unwise—again the Prodigal Son motif (see Introduction). The chief image in this sonnet is that of a person conspiring to put to ruin an entirely beautiful house and family, that person being filled with murderous hatred—for himself! Note that Shakespeare for the first time mentions himself in the first person (9, 13). The word "kind" had associations of gentleness, love, and the keeping of natural law (i.e. not the hoarding of his love but the preserving of his beauty). This is a rather artificial sonnet but with a note of genuine sincerity.

(11)—"as fast as thou . . ."

SUMMARY: *Nature's gift of beauty is to be preserved by passing it on through one's offspring.*

PARAPHRASE

1. As fast as your beauty wanes, so will it
2. increase in your offspring:
3. the fresh blood you give to your child when you are in your prime,
4. may still be called your own when you become old.
5. In offspring live wisdom, beauty and growth:
6. without them there is only folly, old age, and death.
7. If every man believed as you did, the world would end
8. in the mere sixty years of a man's life span.
9. Let those men whom nature has not created to replenish her reserves of beauty

10. perish—harsh, ugly, cruel, without children:
11. whomever nature endowed best, to him she gave even more:
12. you should, by being prolific, increase her gifts.
13.   She created you her model of beauty, intending
14.   that you should create more beauty, and not allow her
     ideal of beauty to perish in time.

> **COMMENT:** Another parable from the New Testament per-
> meating the sonnets is that of the talents (Matthew 25: 14-30;
> see Introduction). Briefly it tells of a young man who does
> not put his inheritance to use, allowing it to remain idle; for
> that, he is strongly reprimanded. The moral is that man's
> endowments of love, mercy, kindness (and here, beauty) are
> useless if left idle. The greater the endowment the more the
> obligation to put them to good use: man is the eternal
> *steward* of his excellences and endowments, and not the
> *owner* of them. Too often such a philosophy was misused by
> greedy capitalists of Shakespeare's day to justify capitalistic
> investment of accumulated and acquired wealth. This was
> particularly true of some Puritans who felt that material
> success was a proof of God's grace.

(12)—"when I do count . . ."

SUMMARY: *When I note that all things eventually shall die and I
realize that you too shall perish in time—then I see that the only
way to defeat the ravages of time is by the begetting of children.*

PARAPHRASE

1. When I observe from gazing at the clock that time causes
2. each beautiful day to turn eventually into hideous night;
3. when I behold decaying violets,
4. and heads of curly black hair becoming streaked with white;
5. when I see the lofty trees turning leafless,
6. which formerly provided shade for the herd,
7. and summer's wheat all tied up in bundles
8. carried on the wagons and showing their white bristly beards—
9. then, concerning your beauty, I speculate
10. that you must inevitably go with the other wasted products of
    time,
11. since all beautiful things eventually forsake their own loveliness
12. and die as fast as other beautiful things arrive to replace them.
13.   And nothing can stand against death
14.   except children to defy him, when Death seizes you.

COMMENT: *Mutability* is the theme of a good many of these sonnets: time is pictured as the inevitable bringer of decay and death, the only way to defeat him being the production of children, which provides a kind of immortality.

Organization: The first four lines (quartain) contain two "*when* statements" declaring that certain beauties, like the day, the violets, and black hair in the process of time lose their beauty. The next quatrain (5-8) makes the same statement about trees and wheat. The third quatrain begins with a *then* clause, signifying the poet's conclusion drawn from the first two quatrains or *octave* (1-8): that his beautiful friend will suffer the same fate, i.e. the loss of his beauty in the mutability of time. The concluding couplet presents the solution to the "problem" of time's mutability: that only production of children can defeat time's destruction of youthful beauty.

Technique: The rhyme scheme (i.e., the pattern of end rhymes) runs:

a (time) b (night) a (prime) b (white)
c (leaves) d (herd) c (sheaves) d (beard); ("beard" is pronounced *bird*)
e (make) f (go) e (forsake) f (grow)
g (fence) g (hence) = a couplet.
The rhythm of the poem follows an alternation of weak and strong accents:
Whĕn í dŏ cóunt thĕ clóck thăt télls thĕ tíme
‿= weak or unstressed beat and ´= a strong or stressed beat. An unstressed syllable followed by a stressed syllable is known as an *iambic foot*. When there are *five* iambs to a line, as here, the line is said to have a rhythm (*meter*) of *iambic pentameter*. In short, then, the *sonnet* of the *Shakespearean type* is a *14 line poem* consisting of three *quatrains* and a concluding *couplet*, all in *iambic pentameter*, with a *rhyme scheme* of abab cdcd efef gg.

Variants in the meter make for *emphasis* of the idea. This sonnet contains a variant in line 2: thĕ *bráve dáy súnk* iñ hídeoŭs níght; *bráve dáy súnk* all receive strong accents for purposes of emphasis; the slowing up of the rhythm and the three long beats make the reader dwell on the awesome beauty of the handsome day "*sunk* (itself containing a sound of hideous finality) in hideous (pronounced híd yŭhs) *night*." "*Past* prime," "green all girded," "*breed* to *brave*," are examples of *alliteration* (repetition of the same initial consonant or vowel) that add to the poetic effect of sound and sense.

(13)—"o, that you were . . ."

SUMMARY: *Only children can preserve family and beauty and withstand death; since your father created you, let your son say the same.*

PARAPHRASE

1. O, if only you forever remained as you are! but, my love,
2. possession of yourself continues no longer than your own lifetime:
3. against death's inevitability you should be prepared
4. by passing on your sweet beauty to someone else.
5. In this way the beauty lent you by nature
6. will be eternal: thus you
7. would live again, even after your death,
8. in that your sweet offspring would preserve and carry on your sweet image.
9. Who would allow so beautiful a family to perish,
10. when it could be preserved, by honorable marriage,
11. against old age
12. and cold, empty death.
13. O, none but spendthrifts! My love, you know
14. you had a father: let your son say the same.

COMMENT: Here for the first time Shakespeare addresses his friend as "my love," an indication of closer intimacy. The reader should keep in mind that addressing friends as lovers was conventional and did not necessarily carry sexual overtones. The conceit that stands out here is that of a houseowner holding a lease on a house (the body as well as family inheritance, etc.), which through good husbandry (thrift, housekeeping, wise care) will keep the property in beautiful shape beauty) (lines 5-10). Note the *custody-of-nature* theme: nature's gifts are to be put to use since man is merely the steward of his own gifts: see Matthew 25:14-30.

(14)—"not from the stars . . ."

SUMMARY: *I tell your fortune by gazing not at the stars but into your eyes, where I read that your truth and beauty will endure only in your offspring; otherwise both will perish at your death.*

PARAPHRASE

1. I do not derive my opinions from star fortune-telling,
2. and yet I think I do know astrology well;
3. but not enough to find in it good or evil luck,
4. future plagues or famines, or the weather to be.
5. Nor can I predict from the stars, in precise detail,
6. what the weather will be like—whether thunder, rain or wind;
7. or foretell for princes whether all will be well,
8. by the frequent reading of the stars in the sky.
9. Rather, I derive my opinions by gazing at your eyes:
10. they are like constant stars to me, in which I read the lesson
11. that—truth and beauty shall thrive in harmony,
12. if you would only cease from admiring yourself and furnish the world with copies of your self in children.
13. Otherwise I predict this of you:
14. your death is truth's and beauty's destruction.

COMMENT: Men of Shakespeare's day were much devoted to astrology: the reading of the stars and their constellations, the planets and their movements, etc., to determine the future. Astrology is still a popular activity, as witness the numerous astrology charts and magazines on sale on the news stands. The conceit, then, is astrological: *plucking judgment* from the stars, good and evil luck, telling fortune, *pointing the stars,* predicting and prognosticating. Shakespeare cleverly uses astrological metaphors to read his friend's fortune by gazing into his eyes.

(15)—"when I consider..."

SUMMARY: *When I see how brief is the span of youth and beauty before time's onslaughts, I then give life to both youth and beauty by celebrating them in my verse.*

PARAPHRASE

1. When I consider that all growing things
2. remain perfect but for a brief moment;
3. that the world is nothing but a stage putting on shows,
4. upon which the stars shed their influence;
5. When I perceive that men like plants are also
6. favored and hindered even by the same sky;
7. boasting in their youthful vigor, declining from their prime,
8. so that their finest period of youth eventually is forgotten:

9. then the thought of this world's ever-changing state
10. recalls you to my eyes in your present most beautiful youth;
11. and I see destructive time combining with decay
12. to change your handsome youth to ugly old age.
13.   And all for love of you I resist time.
14.   As age robs you of youth, I keep renewing it by celebrating
        it in my verse.

COMMENT: Time's ravages, it is said for the first time in the sonnet sequence, can be overcome by Shakespeare's poetry; for the first time we get a new idea: instead of *progeny* to defeat time, there is *art*. Shakespeare seems to have changed his original plans of exhorting his young friend to have children by here proclaiming that his verse will preserve his friend's beauty eternally.

Imagery: Line 3 compares the *world* to a *stage* presenting shows, one of Shakespeare's favorite images. Line 4 uses astrological terms: a person's birthdate was governed by the stars *ascendant* at that time; stars shed their *influence* upon man and his actions, their *comment* (4). One's career was *cheered* and *checked* by the nature of that influence (just as a stage show was cheered and checked by the cries of the audience). Line 5 compares men to *plants* (*sap, cheered* and *checked* by the sky), and men like plants boast in their youthful sap.

Line 11 personifies Time debating or discoursing with Death (like two debaters or conversers) over the issue of the youth's beauty. *Conversers* is the more logical meaning because the two are not opponents; they simply discuss the means of the decay of the youth's beauty. Line 14 is a splendid re-use of the plant image: as time steals the youth's beauty, the poet will *engraft* (create a new bud on the old plant) the beauty of the youth anew by means of his verse. (*Imagery* is the use of vivid pictures for the purpose of making more beautiful or meaningful the bare language of statement. It generally involves the use of *metaphor,* the comparison of one thing to another without the use of "as" or "like", as in the case of a simile. An example of a metaphor is "this huge stage" to refer to the world. *Metaphor.* It is the heart of poetry, and our greatest metaphors are found in the poetry of William Shakespeare.)

Organization: The first two *quatrains* complain about the destruction of time. The *sestet* answers the "problem" of the octave, the *couplet* forming a kind of surprise ending and a triumphant announcement of the solution to the problem. This is the first of the great sonnets.

(16)—"but wherefore..."

SUMMARY: *A child would prove more effective than my verse in preserving your beauty from time's ravages. To have a child of your own is better than having a verse about you or a portrait.*

PARAPHRASE

1. But why not find a better way
2. to defeat old age?
3. And fortify yourself against it
4. by more effective means than by my verse?
5. Now you are at the height of your youth and beauty,
6. and many virgins, still unpregnated,
7. would willingly bear you living children,
8. much more like you than a painted portrait.
9. So will a child, renewing your youth,
10. which neither portrait nor pen can duplicate
11. in inward worth nor outward appearance,
12. make you live in the eyes of man.
13.   To give away yourself in children continues your self,
14.   and you will live on, reproduced through your own skill.

COMMENT: The *conceit* (elaborate comparison) here is that of a painted portrait which is not so good a copy as an actual son. Neither Shakespeare's pen (in verse) nor the pencils of other poets could hope to celebrate his lover's beauty as well as a true copy of it seen in a son: note words like *lines of life, pencil, pupil pen,* and *drawn.* The garden imagery is patently sexual: maidens = unploughed gardens, and living flowers = offspring (6-7).

(17)—"who will believe ..."

SUMMARY: *Men will not believe my description of your beauty as seen in my verse; but a child would give your beauty double life, both in my verse and in him.*

PARAPHRASE

1. Who in the future will believe my verse,

2. if I filled it full of praise for your great worth?
3. —though heaven knows my verse is like a tomb,
4. which conceals the living you, missing half your worth.
5. If I could describe the beauty of your eyes,
6. and in new poetry list all your graces,
7. ages to come would say, "this poet lies:
8. such heavenly beauty never was in man":
9. so would my verses, yellowed in time with age,
10. be scorned as old babbling liars;
11. and my due praise of you be termed a poet's fantasy,
12. the exaggerated lyrics of an old song.
13.   But if some child of yours were alive at that time in the future,
14.   Your beauty should live twice, in the child and in my verse.

COMMENT: Sonnets 1-17 have urged Shakespeare's friend to make himself immortal by bearing children. This is the last sonnet to treat that theme, and it resolves the problem raised in the linked Sonnets nos. 15 and 16: the friend should gain immortality both through progeny (#16) and through being the subject of Shakespeare's verse (#15).

Imagery: Shakespeare's verse is compared to a tomb holding his friend's remains (i.e., memory), lines 1-4.

Great line: "stretched meter of an antique song."

Note: part rhymes with *deserts* (dez árts), but *tongue* imperfectly rhymes with *song* (although some disagree). Shakespeare's claim of power to confer immortality by celebrating individuals in his poetry is an ancient boast. In Number 18 his pride in his poetry becomes full-blown.

(18)—"shall I compare thee . . ."

SUMMARY: *You are more lovely than a summer's day; your beauty will last forever, since it will be given immortality by being praised in my verse.*

PARAPHRASE

1. Shall I compare you to a summer's day?
2. You are more lovely and more gentle of disposition.
3. Rough winds shake the precious buds of May,
4. and summer's stay is all too brief.

5. Sometimes the summer sun is too hot,
6. and often the sun is covered by clouds;
7. everything beautiful declines in beauty, either
8. by chance or by nature's rough conditions.
9. But your beauty, like an eternal summer, shall never fade,
10. nor will it decline in its loveliness;
11. nor shall death wipe out your beauty
12. when your beauty and time's eternity are one and the same.
13.   So long as men breathe and eyes see,
14.   so long will my verse live and give eternal life to you.

COMMENT: This is one of the greatest of the sonnets. The "eternizing" theme is quite clear and offers no difficulties: the youth's beauties will be immortalized in Shakespeare's verse, and time and decay will have been outwitted and defeated. In Sonnet 15 our poet asserted he would *engraft* the youth's beauty in his verse, but now he says he will confer immortality upon the youth through his verse, a subtle change to boasting, which Shakespeare has obviously made good.

Imagery: Line 1 compares the *youth* to a summer's *day* (lovely, temperate). Line 4 is complex: *summer* by implication is a *tenant* holding a lease for a short term, *Time* obviously holding that lease like some kind of eternal *landlord*.

Lines 5 and 6 compare the sun to a person (*eye, complexion*). Line 9 returns to the metaphor of the seasons: the *beauty* of the youth is compared to *summer,* now eternal instead of short-termed Line 11 personifies *Death* as a boasting *person* (he *brags*).

Technique: The iambic pentameter meter has the following primary variants: *Róugh wińds ,* and *Deáth brágs.* Here we find two strong accents to a foot (called a *spondee*). These variants serve to give a more prominent emphasis to those important words. As we can see, the spondee variants in line 11 — "nór shăll|deáth brág|thŏu wánderst iń|hĭs sháde"—slow the pace at the point where the meaning requires such pace; in the foot *"deáth brág ,"* the double emphasis intensifies the picture of boastful and menacing death. Line 4 ends in short, clipped syllables ("hath all too short a date") which give an effect of terse and unsentimental finality to the lease of summer. There are many more metrical effects in this subtle and beautiful poem, but space is lacking here to discuss them all.

Organization: The *first* quatrain proclaims that the youth is better than a summer's day in loveliness, temperance, and longevity. The *second* quatrain explains the possible defects of summer in the erratic behavior of the sun. The *sestet* proudly asserts that in contrast to the summer's day with its uncertain sun, the youth's beauty will survive both summer and death, itself. The *couplet* unfortunately, repeats line 12 and weakens the effect of the three quatrains with its aphoristic generalization. This is the fault of the form of the Shakespearean sonnet. The concluding couplet, like an unwanted tail, reasserts, in more or less *clichéd* terms, what has already been said in the preceding twelve lines.

(19)—"devouring time . . ."

SUMMARY: *Time, do not spoil my friend's beauty; and yet, even if you do your worst, my love will eternally be young in my verse.*

PARAPHRASE

1. Time (which eats up all) makes the lion's paws weak,
2. and makes the earth bury those to whom she gave life;
3. makes the tiger toothless through old age,
4. and burns the immortal phoenix in her own ashes.
5. Makes the seasons happy or sad as you (Time) fly on;
6. and do whatever you wish, swift Time; destroy
7. the wide world and all its fading beauties.
8. But I forbid you one most evil crime:
9. do not put lines of age in the brow of my loved one,
10. nor put wrinkles there;
11. allow him to proceed untouched by age,
12. as a pattern of beauty to future generations.
13. Yet, do your worst, old Time! despite your aging process,
14. my love shall in my verse ever live young.

COMMENT: A conventional theme of the Renaissance is the awful effects of Time, the destroyer of beauty and love. Time, however, can be defeated by one's progeny or by one's fame won by doing good and practising virtue (from Plato). Shakespeare here uses a third way to oppose Time by showing how his art itself can confer immortality. Interestingly, the word "time" occurs seventy-eight times in Sonnets 1-126, and not once more later! (See Hubler's *Shakespeare's Songs and Poems*, p. 24.)

Imagery: Time is pictured as a huge *monster,* fleeting, swift-footed, preying upon the mighty.

Time's *hours* are pictured as *carvers* of lines of age in the brow of Shakespeare's youth (9-10).

Great lines: "O, carve not with thy hours my love's fair brow, Nor draw no lines there with thine antique pen."

(20)—"a woman's face..."

SUMMARY: *You have a woman's beauties and virtues but not her vices; in her fondness Nature added an organ to your beauty which cheated me of you. Then let women enjoy your embraces; I have your spiritual love.*

PARAPHRASE

1. You have a woman's face with a complexion of natural colors,
2. you who are both master of my love and mistress of it;
3. a woman's gentle heart you have, but you are not
4. as changeable as is the habit of false women;
5. your eyes are brighter than women's, more sincere than theirs,
6. shedding light on any object they glance at.
7. You are a man in complexion and nature with all other natures under your command,
8. who attracts men's glances and women's hearts.
9. And as a woman were you first intended,
10. till Nature, while creating you, began to dote on you
11. and defrauded me of you
12. by adding one organ which is of no use to me.
13.   But since she chose you to give pleasure to women,
14.   let your true love be for me and your embraces for them.

COMMENT: This sonnet seems to deny any homosexual intent on Shakespeare's part: true, his friend has a woman's heart and complexion and eyes, but the addition of the male organ made him sexually suitable only for women while Shakespeare enjoyed his true love (friendship). No overt homosexual would speak in this way of his lover. In addition, the plays (as Partridge indicates in his *Shakespeare's Bawdy*) reveal the typical healthy heterosexuality of a normal man. See Introduction for further details.

Note: the *double rhyming* at the end of every line, and observe also the constant use of the *feminine ending* at the end of every line, adding delicacy and softness to the effect. *Pricked = to select* and the *male organ,* a bawdy pun.

(21)—"so it is not . . ."

SUMMARY: *I will not use far-fetched comparisons to describe my love. Let other poets go by hearsay—I shall not exaggerate in order to impress others.*

PARAPHRASE

1. I am not like those poets who,
2. inspired by false beauty to write poetry of praise,
3. call upon heaven itself for comparisons,
4. and use every beautiful thing
5. as a puffed-up metaphor to describe their beloved;
6. such as the sun and moon, the earth, and the sea's beauties,
7. April's first flowers, and everything rare
8. that is to be found on the huge earth, enclosed by the air of heaven.
9. O, let me, true in my love, write truly,
10. and then believe me: my love is as fair
11. as any mother's child, although his beauty is not so bright
12. as the stars.
13. Let other poets exaggerate what they know only from hearsay;
14. I shall not praise you since I am not trying to sell you.

COMMENT: Shakespeare's fellow poets like Sidney, Chapman, and Drayton were overfond of far-fetched conceits and exaggerated praise. This poem strikes a genuine note of sincerity, if not a bit of pique.

Imagery: Except for a few phrases like the *sea's rich gems* and the earth's *huge rondure* (6 and 8) the poem is remarkably free of ornament. Perhaps we have in "Let them say more," a reference to a rival poet who is also addressing poems of praise to Shakespeare's friend. See Introduction on the Rival Poet.

(22)—"my glass shall not . . ."

SUMMARY: *I cannot be older than you, my love, since my heart lives in your breast and yours in mine. When I die in your heart, do not then ask for your heart back.*

PARAPHRASE

1. My mirror cannot convince me that I am old,
2. so long as you and your self are one and the same;
3. but when I shall see you becoming wrinkled by age,
4. then I shall expect soon to die.
5. For all your outward beauty
6. is really the clothing of my heart,
7. which lives in your breast, just as your heart lives in mine.
8. How then can I be older than you?
9. Therefore, my love, take as good care of your self
10. as I will of you, even if not of my self;
11. but since I have your love, I will be as careful of it
12. as a tender nurse protecting her babe from harm.
13.   When my heart is destroyed, ask not for your's in return;
14.   you gave me yours never to take it back.

COMMENT: Shakespeare at around thirty years of age is persuading himself that he is no older than his youthful friend, who is some ten or twelve years younger than he.

Imagery: The conceit is that Shakespeare's image lives in the heart of his friend and *vice versa*. Hence Shakespeare, by identity, shares his friend's youth and age. Clever, but not convincing. We shall find clever games of logic played often in the sonnets, this being a form of wit in which that age delighted. This type of wit develops into a perverse brilliance with Shakespeare's younger contemporaries like John Donne. *Wary* and *chary* are feminine rhymes giving a kind of sly effect (9, 11).

(23)—"as an imperfect actor..."

SUMMARY: *I lack self-confidence in expressing my love; so let my poems express my love more effectively than my tongue.*

PARAPHRASE

1. Like an awkward stage actor,
2. who from fright forgets his part,
3. or who is so stirred with passion
4. that his role becomes less effective:
5. so I, not trusting myself, forget to utter
6. the complete and proper formulas of love;
7. and I seem to weaken in my love,

8. from the strength of too much emotion.
9. O, let my looks then speak eloquently,
10. as silent revelations of my inner feelings;
11. they plead my love and look for love's reward
12. more than can be obtained by speech,
    which has expressed more eloquently of greater loves.
13.   O, learn to read my silent love in verse:
14.   to hear of love through the eyes is part of love's subtlety.

COMMENT: An interesting sonnet: Shakespeare the actor chooses a plain unvarnished simile from his own profession. The comparison is sincere and eloquent. There is still the feeling that Shakespeare is addressing his friend with shyness and diffidence.

Note in line 10, *dumb presagers,* which Hubler says reminds us of the dumb shows that preceded many an Elizabethan play.

Good line: "The perfect ceremony of love's rite."

(24)—"mine eye hath played . . ."

SUMMARY: *Our eyes are windows through which we see each others' love deep in our respective breasts—yet eyes cannot know what the heart is really like.*

PARAPHRASE

1. My eyes, like a painter's brush, have drawn
2. your lovely shape on the canvas of my heart;
3. my body is the frame around your picture,
4. and the perspective given is the art of a supreme painter's.
5. For through my eyes you will detect the skill of that painter,
6. and find where your true portrait lies:
7. it hangs in my bosom as in a painter's shop,
8. with your eyes serving as the shop windows.
9. Now see what good turns eyes for eyes have done:
10. my eyes have drawn your figure, and your eyes act
11. as windows to my breast, through which the sun
12. loves to peep and gaze at your picture there.
13.   Yet eyes lack the skill necessary to art:
14.   they paint only what they see and know not the heart.

COMMENT: The conceit is the most involved and clever one so far. Shakespeare's eyes have seen his friend, taken the reflected image and placed it in the poet's heart, his body serving as a frame for the picture and his eyes serving as the shop windows through which the "portrait" can be seen. The conceit is drawn from painting: eyes = painter, heart = canvas, bosom = shop, eyes = shop windows, sun = onlooker peeping through shop windows. Logically it does not quite hold together, and our poet is caught in being overclever, forced, and inconsistent in his imagery. This type of conceit is characteristic of the technique of the so-called "Metaphysical Poets," Donne, Herbert, Vaughan and Crashaw.

(25)—"let those who are . . ."

SUMMARY: *Unlike princes' favorites who live unsure lives under fickle masters, I love and am loved in return by my master without fear of ever finding fickle change.*

PARAPHRASE

1. Let those favored by good Fortune boast of
2. public honors and titles of nobility;
3. while I, who am barred from such things,
4. take joy unnoticed in those things I honor most.
5. Great princes' favorites, like plants spreading their leaves, enjoy their masters' favor,
6. but, like the marigold, they enjoy that favor only when their masters are pleased;
7. and the cocksure pride of the favorites soon disappears,
8. for at a frown they in their vanity die.
9. The wounded warrior, famous for battles won,
10. after winning a thousand battles and but once a loser,
11. is driven completely from public honor,
12. and all his deeds forgotten for which he toiled.
13.   Then happy me, who love and am loved in return,
14.   and neither love suffers lessening.

COMMENT: We see Shakespeare, the humble actor, scorning the favor of princes for the unceasing love of his friend. Line 3 indicates the estimate then commonly held of actors and playwrights—about on a par with rogues and vagabonds; hence the importance of patronage. Rowse (see Bibliography) believes this sonnet refers to the fall from favor of Sir Walter Raleigh in 1592, which also makes it for him a *dating* sonnet.

Imagery: Most distinctive is the flower imagery of a plant spreading its leaves under the sun's glory and dying under its cloudy disapproval; such is the way with princes and their favorites.

Good line: "from the book of honor raséd quite."

(26)—"lord of my love..."

SUMMARY: *I send these poems, meager as they are, to you, my love, till such time as I am in better favor with Fortune—at which time I shall openly declare my love.*

PARAPHRASE

1. Lord of my love to whom, as your vassal,
2. my sense of duty has been bound firmly by your worth;
3. to you I send this poetic message
4. as a sign of service, not to display my wit.
5. My duty is so great that my poor wit
6. will prove inadequate in its lack of ready words;
7. but I hope that some good opinion of yours
8. will approve my poetic message, bare as it is, in your soul's mind,
9. till that time when my fortune (as seen in the stars)
10. has taken a turn for the better,
11. and allows me to express my love more fittingly,
12. to show me worthy of your respect.
13.   Then will I dare to boast how I do love you,
14.   and until then not reveal the depth of my love.

COMMENT: Shakespeare addresses his patron-friend as a vassal would a lord, and writes this sonnet as a kind of note to accompany "this written ambassage." He is still shy of confidence in his own powers; there is a hint too of bad luck in Shakespeare's own life. One group of scholars think these were the plague years, 1592-1593 when the theaters were closed, barring Shakespeare from a livelihood.

Imagery: Every Elizabethan believed he had a star as a kind of protector; here Shakespeare awaits a favorable "pointing" and fair "aspect" (10) at which time there will be a favorable turn in his fortunes. This again is astrology, of which Shakespeare was so fond.

(27)—"weary with toil . . ."

SUMMARY: *Weary from travel I am yet unable to sleep at night because your face keeps appearing to me.*

PARAPHRASE

1. Weary with toil I hurry to bed
2. to rest my limbs tired with travel;
3. but then my mind's eye
4. becomes active after the body is at rest.
5. For then my thoughts, far from where I lie,
6. make a pilgrimage to you,
7. thus keeping my drooping eyelids wide open,
8. looking into the darkness such as the blind only do,
9. except that my imagination
10. presents your image to my mind,
11. which, like a jewel in the deathlike dark,
12. makes the black night beautiful and glowing.
13.   Lo, thus, my legs at day and my mind at night
14.   obtain no rest because of you.

COMMENT: Shakespeare is evidently traveling, absent from his beloved friend—the first so-called *absence sonnet*. Most, if not all, of the absence sonnets are not too successful. Here the most successful image is that of his friend's image hanging in the darkness "like a jewel hung in ghastly night" (11).

(28)—"how can I then . . ."

SUMMARY: *I find no rest thinking of you, my love, neither while traveling nor in repose.*

PARAPHRASE

1. How can I return to you from travel, in happiness,
2. when I am kept from resting?
3. When the day's weariness is not eased by night,
4. and I am wearied by both day and night?
5. And both, though enemies to each other, combine to interrupt the other's peace,
6. and constantly keep me from rest:
7. the one by work, the other (night) by reminding me
8. how far I am traveling wearily, always farther from you.
9. I tell the day you are bright, in order to please him;

10. and how you make the day brighter when it is cloudy;
11. So I keep flattering the dark night, telling him that
12. when there is an untwinkling, starless sky, your memory brightens it up.
13.   But daylight daily lengthens my sorrow,
14.   and night only strengthens my grief when away from you.

COMMENT: *Absence* sonnets are an Elizabethan convention. This one follows closely upon the preceding sonnet. "Twire" in line 12 could also mean "peer" or "peek."

(29)—"when in disgrace..."

SUMMARY: *At times when I am most depressed and envious of others, the thought of your love always brings me great satisfaction and joy.*

PARAPHRASE

1. When beset by bad luck and in disfavor,
2. I all alone weep over my misery,
3. and pray for help in vain, with useless cries,
4. looking at myself and cursing my fate.
5. Then I wish I had the richer prospects of another,
6. with his looks and his friends;
7. desiring this man's skill and that man's range of abilities;
8. least happy with the talents I am best gifted with.
9. Yet, while in these dismal moods, despising myself almost
10. I happen to think of you, and then my mood,
11. (like a lark rising in the dawn
12. from the dark earth) rises to prayerful thanksgiving.
13.   For your sweet love recalled to mind is equal to such great wealth,
14.   that then I scorn to change my condition with kings.

COMMENT: The Shakespearean editor Malone said of this sonnet that it saves the whole lot from censure (see Rollins edition). But Sir Sidney Lee in his edition said it is nothing but a rehash of conventional Renaissance ideas as found in poets like Petrarch and Tasso. George Whetstone in his *English Mirror* (1586) had similar sentiments: "Yea when affection lead's him to murmure and rage against God . . . reason shall be forced to give place unto force and not let to disgorge blasphemes . . ." (see Rollins edition). There is little artificiality in this sonnet; it is sincere, genuine, and powerful in its stark simplicity. Our poet is bitter and resentful, feels like an outcast, curses his station in life (actor), which was considered of the lowest class.

Rowse thinks the nadir of Shakespeare's life came at the time of the closing of the theaters (1592-3). He was without a livelihood, and making a living was precarious indeed as Robert Greene, Kyd, Peele, and Marlowe had discovered (they all had died in poverty at an early age by this time). Line 8 seems a damaging admission that Shakespeare was contented least with the profession of acting and playwriting, which he, nevertheless, found most enjoyable. *Imagery:* One of the greatest images in the sonnets occurs in line 10-12 where his feelings (*state*) is compared to a lark rising from the dark dawn-lit earth into the sky singing "hymns at heaven's gate." The reader should read this poem along with Sonnets 25, 110, and 111. Hubler (p. 34) thinks Shakespeare bewailed the lack of social acceptance of his profession, but, in addition, his profound pessimism was owing to "his limitations as an artist" since he wrote as one who had not yet become famous.

Organization: Quatrain 1: Shakespeare curses his fate at being in the world as an outcast. *Quatrain 2:* He envies others more fortunate than he. *Quatrain 3:* When at the depths of his pessimism, the thought of his friend raises his feelings to a high pitch of exaltation.

The couplet: The knowledge that he enjoys his friend's love makes him uniquely wealthy. Here the couplet contains the solution to the "problem" of the first two quatrains.

Technique: Variants on the iambic pattern: *Whén iñ, Mén's eyés, deáf heávĕn, súch weálth briñgs,* etc. These changes in the rhythmic pattern give emphasis, weight, and solemnity to the meanings of those phrases.

Like tŏ|thĕ laŕk|ăt breák|ŏf daý|ăríśĭng

A truly great line technically: the phrase *tŏ|thĕ laŕk* has the swiftness of a bird's flight; the word *"arising"* rises and falls like a lark's actual flight in the air.

(30)—"when to the sessions . . ."

SUMMARY: *When alone with my thoughts, I weep afresh over* *past sorrows and griefs; but the thought of you, dear friend, puts an immediate end to my griefs.*

PARAPHRASE

1. When I am pleasurably alone with my own thoughts,
2. I recall to mind memories of past things,
3. and I begin to sigh for many a thing I had longed for;
4. and wail anew over old sorrows, regretting precious time lost.
5. Then do I weep, although unaccustomed to doing so,
6. for beloved friends who have passed away;
7. I weep anew over the memory of forgotten loves,
8. and wail the loss to me again of what many vanished sights have cost me in pain and grief.
9. Then do I grieve again over past sorrows,
10. and recount sorrowfully the number of my past woes
11. over which I had grieved long before, and for which I newly grieve, as if I had never wept over them in the past.
13. But if, during this interval, I think of you, dear friend,
14. then all past losses are restored and all my sorrows are over.

COMMENT: This is one of Shakespeare's greatest sonnets. Shakespeare's phrase *remembrance of things past* became the title of the great modern novel by Marcel Proust. Sir Sidney Lee calls Sonnet 30 "the perfection of human utterance." A controversy over the first line once arose between the great modern reflex psychologist B. F. Skinner and the great historical critic E. E. Stoll: Skinner called the repeated alliteration an "accidental reflex," while Stoll called it incidental and purposeful. Hubler, perhaps our best modern critic of the sonnets, finds the alliteration "heavy" and labored, "recalling but not equaling Poe's 'weary wayworn wanderer' " (p. 36). The line is:
When to the sessions of sweet silent thought.

Biographical critics think (among other things) that line 6 could refer to the untimely death of Shakespeare's young son Hamnet (1596), or to the death of the magnificent Marlowe (1593).

L.5 resembles L.1239 in *Lucrece*: "they drown their eyes."

Thirteen of Shakespeare's sonnets use the concluding couplet as a kind of surprise negation of the preceding three quatrains, and Sonnet 30's couplet is among the most well known in this class; but as already noted, the use of a concluding couplet tended to weaken the powerful effect of the preceding lines;

there is a let-down from the tremendous emotion evoked by imagery and rhythm in the quatrains. This couplet danger is inherent in the form of the Shakespearean sonnet itself. The thirteen sonnets with distinctly weak couplets are 19, 30, 34, 42, 60, 84, 86, 91, 92, 131, 133, 139, 141.

Structure: Quatrain 1: At times when alone the poet laments his past woes and losses. *Quatrain 2:* This is an amplification of the same idea; he laments the loss of dead friends and lost loves. *Quatrain 3:* This, again, repeats the idea beginning with a "then" clause. *Couplet:* This contains the answer to the "problem": the memory of his beloved friend eliminates all sense of loss and pain.

Imagery: The great, often-quoted first two lines compare Shakespeare to a judge of a court in *session summoning* up witnesses (*remembrance*) of the past. The remaining imagery centers around the use of commercial terms to express his feelings: friends are hidden in death's *dateless* (endless, used of documents) *night;* he moans the *expense* of vanished sights; he *tells o'er* (counts,) his past woes as would a bank teller going over his *accounts,* which accounts are continuously *paid* in unending sorrow; in the end all *losses* are *restored.*

(31)—"thy bosom is endeared . . ."

SUMMARY: *My love for you is the summation of all my past friendships as well as the summation of my self.*

PARAPHRASE

1. Your breast contains the total affection for others
2. which I formerly had supposed dead;
3. and in your breast reigns love and all its attendant qualities,
4. and all my love for friends now dead.
5. How many a holy and funereal tear
6. have I shed for the sake of friendship,
7. the claims on my love of dear friends, who now appear
8. as absent ones lying hidden in your breast!
9. You are like a grave where my former loves live again;
10. your breast is like a wall hung with trophies of my past lovers (friends),
11. who gave to you what love I had given them;
12. what they owed me is now yours alone:
13.   their images I had loved so much, I now see in you,

14.   and you, who contain them all, have all of me.

> **COMMENT:**   This poem cannot be read correctly unless the reader is aware that friend and lover were synonymous terms in the Renaissance. The *loves* and *lovers* are those friends who were dear to Shakespeare. For the Renaissance view of friendship, see the Introduction.

(32)—"if thou survive..."

SUMMARY: *After my death please disregard my inferior style in my love poems: read better poets for style, but read mine for the love therein expressed.*

PARAPHRASE

1. If you survive the day of my burial,
2. when base death will have covered my bones with dust,
3. and you by chance again will re-read
4. the inferior poetry of your dead lover; then
5. compare it with the poems of better poets than I;
6. and though my lines be inferior to theirs,
7. keep them in memory of my love, not for their rhyme,
8. which is done much better by more fortunate poets.
9. Then grant me but this loving thought:
10. "Had my friend's inspiration grown better in time,
11. he would have produced better poetry than he had,
12. poetry to rank with that of much better poets.
13.   But since he died, and poets are better than he today,
14.   I'll read their poetry for style and his for love."

> **COMMENT:**   Sonnets 27-32 go together since they deal with absence and low spirits; this one seems to be the dedicative one of the group. The reader must keep firmly in mind that "friend" and "lover," meant the same thing and were without sexual connotation in the Renaissance. Notice the modesty, real or assumed, in Shakespeare, who claims his own poetry to be inferior to the other poets then engaged in writing sonnets. The vogue was especially strong in the early 1590's.

(33)—"full many a..."

SUMMARY: *My love, once in love with me, is now turning to another; yet I love him no less, since even great ones have flaws in their character.*

PARAPHRASE

1. Many a glorious morning sunrise have I seen
2. brighten the mountain peaks,
3. bathing in golden sunlight the green meadows,
4. and giving a golden glow to streams;
5. but soon the sun allows dark clouds to cross
6. his heavenly face, with ugly clouds,
7. which hide the sun from the forsaken world,
8. while it steals unseen to sink in the west.
9. Even so my love, who is my sun, one early morning, did shine upon me
10. with his love;
11. but then, alas, this lasted but for a short time,
12. and, like a cloud, an obstacle arose to mask him.
13.   Yet my love for him is not a whit the less;
14.   if the sun in the sky can be obscured, so can great ones (suns, sons) on earth.

COMMENT: Sonnets 33-47 are reactions to his friend's disloyalty: this is the first of that group. The "region cloud" (12) could have been the Dark Lady who came between Shakespeare and his friend, as is shown in later sonnets. However, in this sonnet, is still a guess ,not a certainty, whether the *region cloud* is the infamous Dark Lady. The first cloud over their friendship appears in this sonnet.

Rhyming effects:......Bb are *false rhymes,* and gg have *feminine endings,* which give a kind of fall in accent in the ending couplet, a low-keyed note of desperation and anguish ending in a groan.

(34)—"why didst thou promise . . ."

SUMMARY: *Your contrition and repentance to me for your betrayal does not cure my disgrace nor does it console me: yet your tears shed for me redeem your former betrayal.*

PARAPHRASE

1. Why did you promise me your full love, like a beautiful day,
2. and make me glory in that confidence without suspicion,
3. and then allow clouds to obscure your love,
4. covering your fine beauty with their foul attentions?
5. It is not enough that you break from them now

6. in order to console my sorrow,
7. for no man can speak well of such consolation as yours,
8. which heals my sorrow but not the disgrace;
9. nor can your shame for your act of betrayal allay my grief,
10. even though you repent, my hurt still exists:
11. the offender's sorrow offers but poor consolation
12. to him who bore the brunt of the offense.
13. And yet—your tears of contrition
14. are enough to redeem your crime.

COMMENT: *Sun* = friend (see also 33), beautiful *day* = the friendship, *cloak* = the prudence Shakespeare should have displayed with his friend. The metaphor continues: *base clouds* = the foul seducer who stole his friend from Shakespeare's side. The whole image is of a man traveling without a cloak, overtaken by ugly clouds which obscure the sun and bring on a gloomy rain, after which the sun reappears to dry the rain on the traveler's face. The couplet (13-14) may appear to be tacked on unconvincingly, as we are not sure that his grief at his friend's betrayal is really allayed; but it may also be seen to demonstrate the strength of the poet's love which is finally touched and his hurt soothed by his beloved friend's tears.

(35)—"no more be grieved..."

SUMMARY: *I both excuse your betrayal and condemn it, like a man with two roles in court: prosecutor and defendant.*

PARAPHRASE

1. Do not grieve any longer at that (your betrayal) which you have committed;
2. roses have thorns, and fountains made of silver contain mud.
3. Clouds and eclipses darken both moon and sun,
4. and in the loveliest flower bud is found the loathsome worm.
5. All men are faulty, and even I am so, by
6. justifying your fault in poetic metaphors,
7. thus corrupting myself, excusing your betrayal
8. and sins even more than necessary.
9. For to your sensual fault I bring in reason—
10. your opponent in this case, pleads your cause—
11. and I start a lawful plea against myself:
12. love and resentment for you clash within me so strongly

13.   that I must act as the fellow-sinner
14.   to that sweet thief who stole you (to my bitterness) from me.

COMMENT: The poem is one of forgiveness for his friend's betrayal of their friendship, but a forgiveness couched in ironic terms: "and loathsome canker lives in sweetest bud" and "myself corrupting, salving thy amiss."

Imagery: legal imagery predominates in lines 5-14: *faults, authorizing, trespass, amiss, adverse party, advocate, commence a lawful plea, accessory;* the whole conceit pictures a trial at court in which Shakespeare is plaintiff (*adverse party*), the defendant's atorney (*thy advocate*), and a plaintiff against himself; thus he is a double plaintiff, a defense attorney, and a defendant because of the love-hate conflict within him. The phrase "sensual fault" in line 9 is significant since it implies that the friend has been untrue to the poet with a woman, possibly the Dark Lady of the later sonnets.

(36)—"let me confess..."

SUMMARY: *We must be careful in public to protect your reputation, for my love is such that your good name is my chief concern.*

PARAPHRASE

1. I know that we are two who must be separate,
2. although our love makes us one;
3. so shall the faults I have
4. be borne by me alone, without your help.
5. In our two loves there is but one common regard,
6. though in our lives there is a spiteful separation,
7. which, though it does not change our love,
8. it does take away from the joyful time we can have together.
9. I can not publicly give you recognition,
10. lest my own regretted fault should bring shame upon you.
11. Nor can you display public kindness for me,
12. lest it lessen your own reputation.
13.   But do not let us separate—my love is such
14.   that, since you are mine, your good repute is also my concern.

COMMENT: There is *unity in division,* says Shakespeare here, repeating a common idea, Platonic in origin. In a world which demands the physical separation of lovers, there can be found, if one searches for it, a spiritual union.

Imagery: the *blots* (3) perhaps refer to Sonnet 35, taken upon himself from his friend's betrayal.

(37)—"as a decrepit father..."

SUMMARY: *The thought of your gifts and virtues, added to my love, fortify me against misery.*

PARAPHRASE

1. As a decrepit father takes delight
2. in seeing his child active and strong,
3. so I, handicapped by bad luck,
4. take all my comfort from the thought of your goodness and loyalty.
5. Whether beauty, birth, wealth, wit,
6. or any of these things, all, or more of them
7. are among the best of your noble qualities,
8. I add my love to those gifts and virtues.
9. Then I no longer feel handicapped, poor, despised,
10. while the picture of your virtues in my mind enables me to share in them so
11. that I am quite content with the abundance of your virtues;
12. and I live by sharing in your glory.
13. Whatever is best for you, I wish for you:
14. such is my wish, which makes me ten times happier.

COMMENT: Shakespeare is still disconsolate at his friend's betrayal, but there is some consolation: Sonnets 37-39 are attempts at mollifying his grief. The *lame* in line 3 refers not to Shakespeare's physical condition but to his social and economic status.

Imagery: the aged *father* taking delight in the youthful deeds of his "active child" is compared with *Shakespeare*, in his decrepit condition, admiring his youthful friend.

(38)—"how can my muse..."

SUMMARY: *You inspire poets like a tenth Muse, and if my verse pleases these experimental times, may you get the praise.*

PARAPHRASE

1. How can my verse lack a subject to write on,

2. while you live, you, who give my verse
3. your self as a theme, one too excellent
4. for every common poet to relate?
5. O, give yourself the thanks, if anything of mine
6. is worth perusal in your estimation;
7. for who is so inarticulate that he is not inspired by you,
8. when you yourself give light to the creative power?
9. Be the tenth Muse, worth ten times more
10. than the old-fashioned nine Muses whom poets invoke;
11. and let the poet who invokes you write
12. verse that will endure forever.
13.   If my slight Muse pleases these experimental days,
14.   let the labor be mine, but yours the praise.

COMMENT: This sounds like a "duty sonnet," given as part of the rite of patronage, and not out of genuine sincerity. The praise, though exaggerated, is clever, but the sentiment smells of fawning, that despicable attitude so often seen between employer and employee. Note Shakespeare's modest estimate of his own verse in the face of so much rival experimentalism.

(39)—"o, how thy worth . . ."

SUMMARY: *Absence from you would be a torment did it not give me leisure to occupy the time with thoughts of love.*

PARAPHRASE

1. How can I with modesty write of your worth
2. when you are yourself the better part of my soul?
3. What can praising myself then do for me,
4. and what is this praise but self-flattery when I praise you?
5. Because of this situation, let us live apart,
6. and let our dear love lose its undivided unity;
7. so that by this separation I may render
8. you that praise which is due to you alone.
9. O absence, what a torment it would be,
10. were it not that my dismal idleness sweetly allows me
11. to spend that time with thoughts of your love,
12. which time and thoughts are so beautifully beguiled;
13.   and in this way you teach me how to make two persons,
14.   by praising the one here, and the other who is absent.

COMMENT: On this occasion, the friend is on a trip; this is an absence duty-sonnet. *Prove* and *love* rhymed in Shakespeare's day (pruhv and luv).

Great line: "To entertain the time with thoughts of love." (line 11)

(40)—"take all my loves..."

SUMMARY: *With difficulty, I forgive your stealing my loved one, even though ill behavior looks well in you.*

PARAPHRASE

1. Take all those I love; yes, take them all:
2. What do you have now more than before?
3. No love at all, my love, that can be called true love;
4. All my love was yours before you took the other loves.
5. Then, if you take my loved one out of love for me,
6. I cannot blame you since you enjoy one that I also love;
7. and yet you are to blame if you deceive me
8. by wilfully enjoying that which you despise.
9. I forgive your robbery, gentle thief,
10. although you steal all I possess;
11. and yet, love knows it is a greater grief
12. to endure harm from a lover than harm from a hater.
13.   Gracious even in sexual actions, you in whom all evil looks attractive,
14.   hurt me with wrongs, yet we must not be foes.

COMMENT: We learn from later sonnets that Shakespeare's friend was seduced by the poet's mistress, and that she became the sexual partner of both men. Although the "household for three," which seems to be implied here brought much grief to Shakespeare, he attempts to rationalize his friend's deception instead of severing the friendship, patronage being vital to his welfare. This is, however, only one of several sound interpretations of this sonnet. J. B. Leishman, for instance, provides a Platonic explanation of the "all my loves" in line 1, these being the loves which occur on the various ascending rungs of the platonic ladder of love. *Usest* (6) means to sexually "use."

Touching line: "Although thou steal thee all my poverty" (10).

Suggestive phrase: "lascivious grace" (13).

(41)—"those petty wrongs..."

SUMMARY: *I can not blame you for being seduced by my mistress, but you ought to refrain from a double breach of faith—for both you and she have been false to me.*

PARAPHRASE

1. Those petty misdeeds of lust that you commit,
2. when I am sometimes unremembered in your heart,
3. befit your beauty and youth,
4. for temptation always follows wherever you go.
5. You are gentle, and therefore to be won;
6. handsome, and therefore to be tempted sexually.
7. And when a woman tempts, what man
8. will leave in disgust until she has seduced him?
9. Ah, me! you might yet forbear from taking my mistress from me,
10. and restrain your lovely and youthful impulses
11. that lead you on in your passion
12. to a double betrayal:
13.   hers, insofar as your beauty tempted her, and
14.   yours, since your beauty has caused you to be false to me.

COMMENT: For the first time we learn what happened to cause the breach between Shakespeare and his friend: the lady had seduced Shakespeare's youth, who too easily succumbed in the betrayal of his friend—for the lady was Shakespeare's mistress before the seduction took place. Shakespeare reproaches the youth gently, but we see that the young friend is selfish and lacks control over his impulses.

(42)—"that thou hast her..."

SUMMARY: *Both my loves in their common betrayal have given me pain, but my consolation is that since my friend and I are one, my mistress consequently loves me alone!*

PARAPHRASE

1. That you have won my mistress is not the sole cause of my grief,
2. even though I loved her dearly;
3. that she has won you is my chief regret,

4. a loss that more deeply affects me.
5. Offending lovers, I do excuse you thus:
6. you do love her because you know I love her;
7. in the same way she betrays me, because she knows I love you,
8. allowing my friend for my sake to test her.
9. If I lose you, my loss is my mistress's gain;
10. and in my losing her, my friend takes up that loss.
11. Both find each other, I lose both of you,
12. and both lay this affliction upon me because of their love for me.
13.   But here is the consolation: my friend and I are one;
14.   then this is a pretty deception—she loves only me!

COMMENT: Although it is partly a rationalization to say that since the friend is really Shakespeare's "other self" the lady in loving the friend really loves Shakespeare, there is much psychological truth in this analysis of wayward human emotion.

In seducing her lover's friend, the lady is partly enacting a lover's revenge against the poet for being untrue to her, transferring her jealousy to him and proving anew her attractiveness, and partly achieving an emotional identification with him in having the same love object.

(43)—"when most I wink..."

SUMMARY: *Only at night do I see your image clearly in my dreams: all days are really nights to me, and vice versa.*

PARAPHRASE

1. When my eyes are most shut, in sleep, then do I see best,
2. for all during the day my eyes look at things without differentiation;
3. but while sleeping, my eyes see you in my dreams;
4. and, mysteriously lighted, my eyes see clearly in the dark.
5. Then you, whose mere image makes bright all other shadows,
6. how much more distinctly would your actual figure be seen
7. in the clear day, with the help of your own actual inner light,
8. when to closed eyes your image is already so clear and shining!
9. How my eyes would be blessed
10. if they saw you in the living day,
11. when even at the dead of night your attractive though dim image
12. is clearly seen by sightless eyes in heavy sleep.

13.   All days are nights till I see you,
14.   and nights are bright days when I see your image in my dreams.

Imagery: *shadow* = image = darkness = form = presence, etc. This ambiguity allows for much wordplay.

(44)—"if the dull substance..."

SUMMARY: *I wish I were not made of water and earth: I should leap like thought itself over the large distances separating us, but, alas, I am not made of thought.*

PARAPHRASE

1. If my heavy dull flesh were turned into thought,
2. the spiteful distance between us could not hold me;
3. for then, in spite of the space between, I should be carried
4. across far distances to where you are.
5. It would not matter then if I were
6. at the farthest place away from you,
7. since nimble thought can leap over sea and land
8. as soon as one thinks of the place where his lover dwells;
9. but, alas, I am not thought itself,
10. able to leap the large miles between us,
11. but—since I am made of earth and water—
12. I must mournfully await my return to your side in due time,
13.   receiving from the slow elements (water and earth) of which I am composed, nothing
14.   but heavy tears, symbols of each other's grief.

COMMENT: The science of Shakespeare's day believed that the universe was composed of four elements: earth and water, the two heavy elements, and air and fire, the two light elements. So, too, it was thought that the body is made up of earth, water, air, and fire, and that human character depended upon which of these elements predominated. Here the heavy (because subject to gravity and space) elements predominate: hence the tears and heavy sorrow. Thought is air and hence free to move swiftly through space, a common Renaissance idea. The subject of this sonnet is continued in Sonnet 45.

(45)—"the other two..."

SUMMARY: *My thought and desire are with you, and I am left* *with my woe, but upon returning they tell me of your good health and I am filled with joy; no sooner do they return, however, than I instantly grow sad again; since thought and desire must instantly make a return trip to you.*

PARAPHRASE

1. The other two elements of my body, insubstantial air and fire,
2. are both with you, wherever I may be:
3. the first (air) is my thought, the other (fire) my desire,
4. both here and there, moving between us with swift motion.
5. When these swift elements are both gone
6. on a tender errand of love to you,
7. my life, being made up of four elements, left with the remaining two—water and earth—
8. sinks down to death, oppressed with melancholy.
9. Until my life's proper composition is recovered
10. by those swift messengers (air and fire) returning from you,
11. who even now are come back, assuring me
12. of your good health, telling me about you.
13. Hearing this news from thought and desire, I am delighted, but
14. then I am forced to send them back to you again and I immediately become sad.

COMMENT: A *duty-sonnet* which completes Sonnet 44 in theme: when earth and water predominate, the result is melancholy in the individual. See Sonnet 44 commentary.

(46)—"mine eye and heart . . ."

SUMMARY: *In a court trial over the possession of your image, the decision is that my eyes are awarded your outward body and my heart your true love.*

PARAPHRASE

1. My eyes and heart are engaged in a deadly battle
2. as to how to divide the spoils consisting of your image.
3. My eyes would forbid my heart your image,
4. and my heart would forbid the eyes that privilege.
5. My heart pleads that you are contained within it—
6. a closet never pierced with human eyes—
7. but the defendant (eyes) denies the heart's plea,
8. and states your beautiful likeness belongs to him.

9. To decide the case, a jury
10. of thoughts is impanelled—all of them presiding within the heart—
11. and their verdict will decide
12. the case between my clear eyes and my dear heart
13.   in this way: my eyes are awarded your outward body
14.   and my heart your true, inner love.

COMMENT: A favorite game of the Renaissance: the war between eye and heart over possession of the image of the lover, a well-worn cliché by the time Shakespeare adopts it. The conceit of the courtroom is also a cliché, but here it is used with admirable—if forced—ingenuity.

Imagery of the courtroom is created by such words as *bar, right, plead, defendant, plea, deny, impanelled, quest, verdict, moiety, part.* Such legal action for a share of something (usually property) is called an *action for partition.*

(47)—"betwixt mine eye . . ."

SUMMARY: *By sharing your picture between my eyes and heart you are always with me—or if they should fall asleep, the sight of your picture joyfully awakens them.*

PARAPHRASE

1. An agreement is formed between my eyes and heart,
2. and each does good turns now for the other:
3. when my heart is starving for a look at you,
4. or my heart, in love with you, smothers itself in sighs,
5. then my eyes feast upon my love's picture,
6. inviting my heart to feast along with him;
7. another time my eyes are my heart's guest,
8. sharing in my heart's thoughts of love.
9. So, either by your picture or by my love,
10. you are with me always, even though apart;
11. for you are no farther away than my thoughts can travel,
12. and I am with my thoughts and they with you.
13.   Or if they are sleeping, your picture before me
14.   awakens my heart to the joy of both my eyes and heart.

COMMENT: Evidently the legal suit of Sonnet 46 has been settled by the friend's sending a picture of himself to Shakespeare while they are separated by travel. (Could it have been a Hilliard miniature?) This sonnet is a kind of *antiphon* or answer to Sonnet 46.

(48)—"how careful was I..."

SUMMARY: *You are subject to the "raids" of others, even though I have locked you within my heart—for even from within my heart I fear you shall be stolen from me.*

PARAPHRASE

1. How careful I was when I started on my journey,
2. to put each trifle in safe-keeping,
3. so that to my use alone they would remain, untouched
4. by thieves, in trusted safety.
5. But you, compared to whom my jewels are but trifles,
6. my most trusting comfort but now my greatest grief—
7. my dearest love and only interest—
8. are left the prey of every common thief.
9. You, I have not been able to lock up in any jewel box,
10. except where you are not (though I feel you are)
11. within the gentle enclosure of my breast,
12. from which place you may come and go as you please.
13. And even from there you will be stolen, I fear,
14. for even honesty turns thief for such a prize as you.

COMMENT: Sonnets 48-66 form a rough kind of group in which Shakespeare is filled with melancholy over his friend's betrayal. Shakespeare in this group also seems to be on a journey.

Imagery: Shakespeare pictures his breast as a jewel box in which lies the treasure of his love, a treasure which can be stolen by any common thief. The meaning may be that another poet is bidding for his friend's approval by writing *praise-sonnets* akin to those of Shakespeare.

(49)—"against that time..."

SUMMARY: *When the time comes for you to love me no longer, I shall say you are right in doing so, since you are not obligated to go on loving me.*

PARAPHRASE

1. In anticipation of that time (if ever it come)
2. when I shall see you frown at my faults,
3. when your love for me is summed up and ended,
4. called to account after careful reflection by you.
5. In anticipation of that time when you will pass me like a stranger,
6. scarcely greeting me even with your eyes,
7. and when your love for me, changed from what it was,
8. finds weighty reasons and excuses for your unfriendliness:
9. In anticipation of that time I fortify myself
10. with the knowledge of my own worth,
11. and raise my hand in witness against myself,
12. and swear, to my own harm, that your disowning of my love was just.
13.   You have every right to leave poor me
14.   since I can find no lawful obligation for your loving me.

COMMENT: This is a very good sonnet—tender and tinged with sorrow. The very delicate relations between the older and younger man, one born in the lower ranks, and the other proudly and nobly born, could at any time have been definitely severed, had not Shakespeare shown the extreme tact and humanity for which he is so famous. Here in three great "against that time" phrases he prefigures a rejection, and in the fine conceit of a law court swears painfully but nobly that he has no rights in his beloved friend.

(50)—"how weary do I..."

SUMMARY: *My horse and I groan, he from the pricking of my spurs, and I at the distance which separates us.*

PARAPHRASE

1. How sadly do I journey on my way,
2. when what I seek—the end of my weary journey—
3. tells me after reaching a place of rest and comfort
4. "I am so many miles away from my friend."
5. My horse, tired with my woe,
6. plods slowly on, bearing my inner heaviness of spirit,
7. as if by some instinct he knows
8. that his rider dislikes speed, since it makes us more distant from each other at every step.

9. Even the bloody spur cannot stir him on
10. when I sometimes angrily prick his hide;
11. and he answers my pricks with groans,
12. which hurts me more than my spurs did the horse.
13.   For that same groan reminds me
14.   that sorrow is before me, and you, my joy, behind.

COMMENT: Here we have a simple, homely picture of Shakespeare slowly journeying on his reluctant and groaning horse—even a bit comic in its picture of groaning man and beast. Nevertheless, this sonnet is a welcome relief from the forced ingenuities of many of the duty-sonnets.

(51)—"thus can my love . . ."

SUMMARY: *On the return trip to you, no horse would or could keep pace with my eagerness to see you again.*

PARAPHRASE

1. So you can, my love, excuse the offensive slowness
2. of my horse while I journey away from you:
3. from where you are, why should I hurry away?
4. Until I return, there is no need for hurry.
5. But what excuse will my poor beast find,
6. when extreme speed can only seem slow?
7. Then would I give my horse the spur, and even if my horse were the wind
8. and flew so rapidly that I would be aware of no motion;
9. then no horse could keep pace with my desire to rejoin you;
10. therefore desire, born of my perfect love for you,
11. shall be aroused in me (it being not born of dull flesh) and make a fiery dash towards you.
12. But love, for the sake of love, will excuse my nag,
13.   since intentionally he went slowly when leaving you,
14.   in returning to you, I shall run and let my horse jog along by himself.

COMMENT: This sonnet continues the preceding one. Again we have the comic horse plodding beneath a panting lover. We may also see reference to the four elements of Renaissance science here. Desire, being composed of fire, can fly like the wind, while the dull elements of which the flesh is composed must jog along. This opposition of *spirit* and *flesh* is a frequently recurring theme in the sonnets. This sonnet may also be considered a duty-sonnet and is a member of a group of absence sonnets.

(52)—"so am I as the rich..."

SUMMARY: *Time keeps you in his treasure chest, and when it is opened up, I triumph to see you there; and when not by your side I hope to see you there again.*

PARAPHRASE

1. So I am like a rich man whose blessed key
2. opens for him his sweet locked-up treasure,
3. which he will refrain from surveying at every hour,
4. in order not to dull the keener pleasure of more sparing observations.
5. That is why feasts are so ceremonious and rare,
6. since, happening so seldom in the year,
7. they occur as widely spaced as the finest jewels in a necklace.
8. So in the same way Time keeps you as my treasure-chest;
10. or like a wardrobe hiding a cloak,
11. to make some special moment of time especially blessed
12. by opening the treasure chest proudly and revealing you there inside.
13.   Thus you are blessed, whose virtue has such power
14.   that your presence is a victory, and your absence brings the hope of seeing you once again.

COMMENT: *Key* (1) rhymes with *survey*. See Sonnet 48 for a similar idea about a locked chest.

Imagery: Shakespeare compares himself to a *rich man* who refrains from gazing at his treasure too often in order not to decrease his viewing pleasure when he does gaze at it. Clever and ingenious, but unconvincing.

Memorable: "For blunting the fine point of seldom pleasure" and captain jewels in a carcanet"—what magic in that word *captain!*

(53)—"what is your substance..."

SUMMARY: *You are a part of all things lovely, but there is nothing to compare with your constancy in love.*

PARAPHRASE

1. What is your basic element, of what are you made,
2. that millions of strange shadows wait upon you?
3. Everyone has but one shadow,
4. yet you—one person—can lend shadows to all.
5. Describe Adonis, and the description
6. is a poor copy of you;
7. On Helen's cheek set all the arts of loveliness,
8. and it would look like a new painting of you in Grecian attire.
9. Speak of spring and harvest:
10. the one (spring) is but a shadow of your beauty, and
11. the other resembles your own sweet generosity;
12. you are known to us in all your blessed guises;
13.   You have a share in all external graces,
14.   but there is no one like you for constancy in love.

COMMENT: This poem is a tribute to his friend's great generosity. Was the poet given some generous gift by his patron? Evidently so. The use of Adonis (most beautiful of the Greek mythological youths) and Helen of Troy (the fairest of all in Homeric times) are standard comparisons; yet this sonnet breathes a greater sureness on Shakespeare's part— unlike the uneasiness and sterile artificiality of some of the former sonnets. As in Sonnets 99 and 113 we find the common sonnet theme that a poet's beloved lends his beauty to other beautiful things in nature. A neo-Platonic idea is expressed here: that all matter is but a reflection of the *eternal Idea* in the mind of God. In these terms, his friend is something like that eternal Idea. Some critics believe that the perfect friend reflected here could not be the sensual betrayer of the earlier Sonnets 41 and 42.

(54)—"o, how much more . . ."

SUMMARY: *Dog-roses can imitate genuine roses except for their odors; but your beauty can be distilled in my verse when your beauty fades.*

PARAPHRASE

1. O, how much more lovely does beauty seem
2. when truth embellishes it!
3. The rose looks lovely, but we consider it more lovely

4. for the sweet odor it gives off.
5. The dog-roses have as deep a color
6. as the perfumed color of genuine roses.
7. The dog-roses also have thorns and toss prettily
8. when the summer wind opens their buds.
9. But their only virtue is in their appearance,
10. for they live unadmired and unesteemed, and
11. die all alone. But lovely roses do not die in that manner;
12. for the sweetest perfumes are made from the sweet corpses of genuine roses.
13. And in your case too, beauteous and lovely youth,
14. when your beauty fades, my verse will preserve its essence.

COMMENT: Dog-roses could be roses eaten away internally by rose worms. See Sonnets 35, 70, 95, and 99. Here *distill* does not carry the procreative sense it does in Sonnet 6. It means "purify," "condense," abstract." Again Shakespeare promises his patron immortality in verse. A lovely sonnet.

Memorable: "Of their sweet deaths are sweetest odors made."

(55)—"not marble..."

SUMMARY: *Your praise shall outlast wars, fires, and sword: death itself will be outdone! Till the Day of Judgment you will live in my verse and in the eyes of lovers who read this verse.*

PARAPHRASE

1. Neither marble nor the gilded monuments built as memorials
2. to princes can outlast my powerful verse;
3. and you shall be memorialized more brightly in my verse
4. than in memorial tablets of unswept stone dirtied with age.
5. When destructive war shall overturn statues,
6. and battles destroy buildings,
7. neither sword nor fire shall ever burn
8. the living record of your memory.
9. Defying death and inimical oblivion,
10. you shall go on: praise of you will be seen
11. even in the eyes of all posterity, and you
12. will endure until the Judgment Day.
13. So, until the Day of Judgment, when you shall ascend into heaven,
14. you shall live in this, my verse, and live also in the eyes of future lovers who will read my poems.

COMMENT: This is one of the great sonnets expressing the poet's bold conviction that his poetry will defeat time itself. Formerly Shakespeare had been quite modest about the power inherent in his verse; here he declares in almost hymn-like incantations that it is immortal. The announcement was prophetic. But then, it might be said that all true prophets are poets and many poets truly prophetic. The couplet, with its jigging rhyme, obviously weakens what had already been powerfully stated in the three quatrains. Each quatrain declares in separate powerful images that this poetry shall outlive marble, monuments, war destruction, and death itself, up to the very Judgment Day, when Christians (and Shakespeare was a devout Christian) felt that Christ would descend to earth and destroy all his enemies, all sinners, all those who would not recognize Him as Messiah. On his throne in heaven he would then judge the dead and living, consigning each to his proper reward or punishment. The end of the world would be eternal bliss for the Christian faithful and eternal hellfire for the wicked. One possible source of the imagery in the poem is Ovid's *Metamorphoses,* one of Shakespeare's favorite books, which speaks of destructive fire and sword. In the Golding translation (Golding, Shakespeare's contemporary translated Ovid into English and it is this version Shakespeare very likely used) this is rendered as follows: "Now have I brought a work toe end which neither *Jove's* fierce wroth, Nor swoord, nor fyre, nor freating age with all the force it hath are able to abolish quyght." The immortality conceit was a Renaissance convention, widely found in such authors as Ronsard, Spenser, Daniel, Drayton, Du Bellay, Sidney, and Nashe, any of whom may have been Shakespeare's source. Although one critic thought the sonnet "clearly second-rate, if not a third-rate" poem and another thought it not "quite intelligent enough to be metaphysical," the critical consensus is that this is one of the truly great sonnets.

Imagery: "Sluttish *time*" (4) is compared to a *person* who makes filthy the objects with which he comes in contact; there are associations in the word of sexual degeneracy and prostitution. "The living record of your memory" compares *memory* to a *book* of entries, as in a law ledger, a ledger that neither sword, nor fire, nor war can destroy. " 'Gainst death and all-oblivious enmity/Shall you pace forth" (9-10) is a powerful image: his friend issues forth from the ravages of time and death in future ages via the agency of our poet's powerful rhyme. Ruins of architecture often hold a fascination for Shakespeare, as here. See also Sonnet 73. The images of the final couplet are sterile in comparison.

(56)—"sweet love, renew..."

SUMMARY: *Do not let my love sink into apathy in this sad interval of parting, but rather call it a winter which makes summer's coming that much more desirable and rare.*

PARAPHRASE

1. Sweet soul of love, renew your power: let it not be said
2. that your power is weaker than that of sexual desire,
3. which today is satisfied by feeding,
4. but tomorrow remains unsatiated.
5. So, love, be like desire in that respect: although today
6. you satisfy your desire to the utmost,
7. tomorrow require satisfaction again; and do not kill
8. the spirit of love with a constant apathy.
9. Let this sad interval be like the ocean,
10. which divides the shore, where two newly engaged
11. lovers come daily to the banks, so that
12. a repetition of their love may make the view still more lovely.
13.   Or let this sad interval of time away from you be
      like the winter, which, being full of worry,
14.   makes the coming of summer triply more rare and desirable.

COMMENT: There is a hint here of a lack of interest on the part of Shakespeare's friend. But this sonnet is primarily an analysis of the nature of passionate love which requires some obstruction to keep its interest whetted because too frequent meetings tend to dull love's pleasure.

Imagery: The *sad interim* is compared to a *body of water* separating two shores on which stand two divided lovers, a not too successful comparison.

(57)—"being your slave..."

SUMMARY: *I keep thinking of you to while away the tedious hours when you are gone, and, though you may do good or ill, love never thinks ill of you—so devoted a fool is he.*

PARAPHRASE

1. Being your slave, I have nothing to do but wait
2. upon the hours and times of your wishes.
3. My time is not valuable,
4. nor do I have services to perform unless you command them.
5. Nor do I dare scold the tedious hours,
6. while I, my lord, watch the clock for you;
7. nor dare I think absence is bitter,
8. once you have bid your servant (me) adieu.
9. Nor do I dare to question jealously
10. where you may be nor pry into your affairs.
11. But like a sad slave I think of nothing,
12. except that wherever you may be you are making someone happy.
13. Such a fool is love that whatever your desire may be or whatever you may do,
14. he thinks no ill of anything.

COMMENT: *Will* in line 13 is spelled *Will* in the original Quarto of 1609 and could mean Will(iam) Shakespeare, in which case the sense of the whole is that "love makes me such a fool that I think nothing bad no matter what you may do." Sonnets 57 and 58 are quite servile in spirit, a couple of *duty-sonnets* in the worst sense.

(58)—"that God forbid . . ."

SUMMARY: *You may do what you will with your time while I suffer your absence; yet I must wait and suffer, no matter what you may be doing to amuse yourself.*

PARAPHRASE

1. May God forbid, who made me first your slave,
2. that I should in thought try to control your pleasurable activities,
3. or beg an accounting of how you spend your time,
4. since I am your vassal, waiting on your command.
5. Being at your beck and call, let me suffer
6. in my prison at your absence, while you are freely roaming;
7. I tame my impatience with endurance, and take every rebuke
8. without accusing you of hurting me.
9. No matter where you are, the liberty I grant you is so strong

10. that you may spend your time
11. as you please; it is your right
12. to be able to excuse yourself for your own crimes.
13.   I wait for you, though this waiting is hell for me;
14.   and I do not criticize your amusements, be they good or bad.

COMMENT: See Sonnet 57 commentary.

(59)—"if there be nothing..."

SUMMARY: *I wonder what ancient times would say of your perfection; nevertheless, I am sure there has been no better subject to write about.*

PARAPHRASE

1. If there is nothing new on earth but only that which is
2. and has been here before, then how our brains are fooled—
3. trying to create new things—to give birth improperly
4. to the same child already born!
5. O, if only memory could with a backward look
6. of five hundred years,
7. show me your image in some antique book,
8. since thought was first expressed in writing;
9. so I could read what the ancients could say
10. at the sight of the perfection of your figure;
11. whether our times or ancient times are better;
12. or whether the cycle of years is always the same.
13.   I am sure of one thing: the wits of ancient days
14.   have awarded praise to worse subjects than you.

COMMENT: The theme is based on Ecclesiastes, 1:9ff.: "The thing that hath been it is that which shall be; and that which is done is that which shall be done: and there is no new thing under the sun."

Here the cyclic theory of history (a common concept) is questioned—but see Sonnet 123 where Shakespeare accepts it.

(60)—"like as the waves..."

SUMMARY: *Nothing can resist time's call to death, but my verse which will go on praising your virtue and worth.*

PARAPHRASE

1. Like the waves traveling to the pebbled shore,

2. so do the minutes of our lives hasten to their end;
3. each changes place with what is before it,
4. moving forward in measured sequence.
5. the newly born, at first appearing in full light,
6. crawls to maturity and when in his prime
7. malignant forces war against his state,
8. and Time, who gave birth, youth, glory now takes it away.
9. Time takes away the bloom of youth
10. and gives youth wrinkles;
11. it feeds on the rarities of nature's ideal forms,
12. and nothing can resist his call to death.
13.   And yet 'til future time my verse will endure in hope,
14.   Praising your worth—notwithstanding Time's cruelty.

COMMENT: Most criticism agrees that this is a great sonnet. The theme is the commonplace one of *mutability,* the universal transitoriness of all things. Time destroys beauty, but the poet's verse can outlive time itself, another Renaissance idea.

Source: Ovid's *Metamorphoses* (Golding translation) provides a possible source for 1-4:

> As every wave drives other forth
>   and that that comes behind
> Both thrusteth and is thrust itself:
>   Even so the times by kind
> Do fly and follow both at once,
>   and evermore renew.

see the Golding translation as found in Rouse, *Shakespeare's Ovid,* pp. 298:99:

> "Things eb and flow, and every shape is made too passe away.
> The tyme itself continually is fleeting like a brooke.
> For neyther brooke nor lyghtsomme tyme can tarrye
>   still. But looke
> As every wave dryves other foorth, and that that
>   commes behynd
> Bothe thrusteth and is thrust itself: Even so the tymes
>   be kynd
> Doo fly and follow bothe at once, and evermore renew.
> For that that was before is left, and streyght there dooth
>   ensew
> Another that was never erst. Eche twincling of an eye
> Dooth chaunge."

Baldwin believes that Shakespeare borrowed *directly* from

the Ovidian Latin rather than from Golding. If so, his knowledge of Latin was certainly not "smal," as Ben Jonson, a playwright contemporary with Shakespeare, said it was.

Structure: Quatrain 1: Minutes as they occur in time are compared to *waves* rippling towards shore, each ripple inexorably following the ripple before it, just as minutes follow each other inexorably. *Quatrain 2:* The new-born child when grown to maturity is opposed to "crooked eclipses" (7) which battle against his good fortune in the world. Belief in astrology stated that certain eclipses affected man's condition in a malignant way. *Quatrain 3: Time* (9) pictured as a *giver* of gifts of beauty and youth to man, becomes an Indian-giver and demolishes (*confounds,* 8) his gift by *delving* (10) *parallels* of wrinkles (note the likeness to the ripples of waves in line 1) in the brow of youth. In line 12 Time, with his scythe, mows down wheat just as youth is cut down by old age. The personification of Time as a farm labourer in a wheat field is conventional. *In sum:* the three quatrains picture the inevitable destruction of youth by Time, and the couplet, with much less poetic effectiveness, neatly answers the problem by asserting that verses will escape the inevitable scythe of Time.

(61)—"is it thy will . . ."

SUMMARY: *My love for you makes me restless at night, but you are awake elsewhere busied with other companions.*

PARAPHRASE

1. Is it your desire that your image should keep open
2. my heavy eyelids throughout the night?
3. Do you desire my sleep to be interrupted
4. while images resembling you keep haunting me?
5. Is it your ghost that you send
6. so far from home to pry into my deeds,
7. to pry into my faults and idlenesses—is this
8. the aim and purpose of your suspicious nature?
9. O no, your love, though considerable, is not so strong as all that!
10. It is my own love for you that keeps me awake
11. and cheats me of rest, and makes me
12. play the role of watchman because of you.
13.   I keep watch for you, while you are awake elsewhere,
14.   far from me, with others much too near.

COMMENT: There is indicated quite clearly here the differences in the quality of the two lovers: Shakespeare, the truer lover, is jealously suspicious as his beloved unfaithfully cavorts with others—a sad situation indeed. Note the almost Anglo-Saxon simplicity of the vocabulary, an indication of a basic sincerity.

(62)—"sin of self-love . . ."

SUMMARY: *I am guilty of self-love but my mirror tells me otherwise; for it is your self in me that I am really praising.*

PARAPHRASE

1. I am guilty of the sin of self-love in eye,
2. mind, and in every part of my body;
3. and for this sin there can be no cure,
4. since it is based deep within my heart.
5. I think there is nowhere a face so pleasing as mine,
6. no figure so well-shaped, no one so loyal;
7. I put such a great value on my own worth
8. that I think it surpasses all others.
9. But when my mirror shows me as I am,
10. weather-beaten and seamed with leathery old age,
11. then I realize the paradox of my own self-love:
12. for one's self to love self so is evil,
13.   but it is you, my other self, I praise when I praise myself,
14.   thus attributing to my self, your youth and beauty.

COMMENT: The modesty Shakespeare expresses at the close of this sonnet is, perhaps, a mask for the vanity, but it may also be looked on as a lesson in disillusionment earlier asserted. The hem of *unity in oneness* (see Sonnets 22 and 26) appears here again. Actually Shakespeare, as we have said, could have been no more than thirty years of age, but the youth was at least a dozen or so years younger.

Good lines: "grounded inward in my heart"
                 "Beated and chopped with tanned antiquity."

(63)—"against my love . . ."

SUMMARY: *I prepare for that time when age shall steal my love's beauty and life by keeping his memory green in my poetry.*

PARAPHRASE

1. In provision for the time when my love shall be as I am now,
2. crushed and worn out with age,
3. pale and bloodless, and with
4. wrinkled brow; when his youth shall
5. have become old age,
6. and all those youthful charms he now enjoys
7. shall be going or gone from him,
8. gradually and unawares, leaving him without his rich youth;
9. in provision for that day I now take measures
10. against the cruel ugliness of age,
11. so that it never shall leave unremembered
12. my sweet love's beauty even though age take his life.
13.   His beauty shall live on in these black lines of ink,
14.   which will last and keep the memory of his beauty fresh.

COMMENT: Again, as in the preceding sonnet, Shakespeare compares his own age with his beloved's youth, this time, however, not to grant himself a spurious youth through the emotional identification of love but to promise his beloved an immortal youth through the anticipated immortality of his poetry.

(64)—"when I have seen..."

SUMMARY: *Time will eventually take, as it does all things, my love away from me; but this thought is as death to me.*

PARAPHRASE

1. When I have seen how Time's cruel action has defaced
2. proud, expensive monuments of old times;
3. when I see formerly lofty towers torn down,
4. and the everlasting brass tombs subject to death's decay;
5. when I have seen the hungry ocean making inroads
6. farther and farther upon the ocean shore;
7. and the firm ground itself reaching into the sea,
8. increasing gain with loss and loss with gain;
9. when I see such an exchange of conditions—
10. or even states themselves fallen into ruin—
11. then decay and ruin has taught me to reflect thusly:
12. that Time will come and take my love away.
13.   This reflection is like death to me who cannot choose
14.   but weep to know I must eventually lose my love.

COMMENT: In this great sonnet, *mutability* is shown to be triumphant over architecture, over the shifting earth and sea, and over love itself, a fact which endows even the dearest moments of love with poignancy. This sonnet is the climax of a group discussing the *ravages of time*. Rowse (p. 131) finds it historical; Englishmen of the latter half of the sixteenth century saw many historical ruins, "the abbey-towers thrown down by the Reformation, the splendid brasses ripped out of the churches by the fury of the Reformers and the avarice of others." *The Rape of Lucrece* which was perhaps written about the same time as this sonnet contains the following lines: (11.944-45)

> To ruinate proud buildings with thy hours,
> And smear with dust their glittering golden towers.

There also was interest in ruins because 1) the antiquities of Rome were in a process of rediscovery begun at the end of 15th century and 2) the ancient poets who were fond of the theme of ruins and mutability were being revived and read. The expression "brass eternal" is from Horace's *aere perennius,* which Baldwin believes to have been taken from the original Latin (p. 273). Another parallel can be found in Shakespeare's own *Richard II* (III, 2, 160-70):

> for within the hollow crown
> That rounds the mortal temples of a king
> Keeps Death his court and there the antic sits,
> Scoffing his state and grinning at his pomp,
> Allowing him a breath, a little scene,
> To monarchize, be fear'd and kill with looks,
> Infusing him with self and vain conceit,
> As if this flesh which walls about our life
> were brass impregnable, and humor'd thus
> Comes at the last and with a little pin
> Bores through his castle wall, and farewell king!

The quotation provides a splendid picture of Death and Time and the reduction even of monarchs to their sway. Death is an ally of Time in his ravages. *Measure for Measure,* V, 1, 9-13 contains a similar image:

> O, your desert speaks loud; and I should wrong it,
> To lock it in the wards of covert bosom,
> When it deserves, with characters of brass,
> A forted residence 'gainst the tooth of time
> And razure of oblivion.

Structure: Quatrain 1: Time destroys great buildings and brass (considered especially durable) tablets. *Quatrain 2:* The ocean in the process of time steadily takes away from the earth itself. *Quatrain 3* reflects on this with the deduction that Time will do the same to his beloved friend. The concluding couplet pictures the reactions of the poet to this thought: that time in its inevitable progress will destroy his friend.

Imagery: *Time* is pictured as an evil, destructive *person* (*fell hand,* 1) who will take his love away (12).

Technique: The strong stresses on *Time's fell hand* (1) changing the iambic pattern to spondees, gives great stress and tension to the concept of Time's evil hand, an example of variant stress that enforces meaning. There are many other variants too numerous to detail here.

(65)—"since brass, nor stone . . ."

SUMMARY: *Only in my poetry will my love's memory be kept fresh in the face of time's ravages.*

PARAPHRASE

1. Since brass, stone, earth, and boundless seas
2. are all subject to death,
3. then how in the face of death through time can beauty keep its freshness and hold out,
4. whose own strength is no greater than that of a flower?
5. O, how shall the sweet lovely summertime hold out
6. against the continual ruin of Time,
7. when even impregnable rocks are not mighty enough,
8. nor steel gates themselves strong enough to stand against Time's decay.
9. O fearful thought! How then, alas,
10. shall you, Time's best jewel, be hidden from the coffin of Time's chest?
11. Or who can resist the swift progress of Time
12. or prevent Time from ravaging and despoiling beauty?
13.   O, none can, unless the power of my miraculous pen
14.   shall in black ink make my love ever shine bright.

COMMENT: This sonnet continues the theme of Sonnet 64, but with the difference that here the ravaging effects of Time are defied through the immortalizing power of poetry.

Imagery: Quatrain 1: Beauty is compared to an innocent youth pleading mercy against Death (*sad mortality*, 12). *Quatrain 2: Summer* is pictured as a sweet, honey-breathed *youth* attempting to *hold out* (the association implies a surrounding or besieging of the youthful summer) against the *days* (here pictured as a besieging *army*). *Quatrain 3: Time* is pictured as the *owner* of a chest (a coffin) into which he crams all the finest jewels on earth (i.e., beautiful youths); in addition he is pictured in line 12 as preying upon beauty and despoiling it. The association here is of rape or attack. The *couplet* answers the problem stated in the quatrains: his verses will immortalize the youth's beauty.

(66)—"tired with all these..."

SUMMARY: *With good so subject to evil in this world I prefer death to life—except that in death I leave you alone.*

PARAPHRASE

1. Weary with the thought of all these things,
   I cry for the peace of death:
2. when I behold those deserving reward born as beggars,
3. and worthless people arrayed in finery,
4. and purest faith evilly betrayed,
5. and great honor paid to the unworthy,
6. and innocent virtue made vile,
7. and the truly good banished from favor,
8. and strength weakened by poor leadership,
9. and art made ineffective by censorship and power,
10. and stupidity owlishly controlling the artist,
11. and plain truth looked on as simple mindedness,
12. and good subjected to powerful evil.
13.   Weary with all these thoughts, I would rather be dead,
14.   except that in dying, I leave my love alone.

COMMENT: A great sonnet yet, oddly, seldom quoted by the layman. Shakespeare, in angry despair, lashes out at all civilized vice and stupidity. It is certainly one of the most personal and revealing of all the sonnets, and quite indicative of his chief targets in the plays, as for example in Hamlet's "to be or not to be" soliloquy. The rhyme scheme is in the sonnet mold, but note that the structure is not arranged in the usual triple quatrain form, and, except for the first two lines and the last two, the entire poem begins each line with the word "and" as if to imply that the series of wrongs, injuries, insults, and asininity is endless.

(67)—"ah, wherefore with infection . . ."

SUMMARY: *My love spends his time in sin and imitation, violating his natural beauty, but he is Nature's only supply of beauty left in these evil times.*

PARAPHRASE

1. Ah, why should he go on living in corruption,
2. gracing it with his presence,
3. giving it the advantage of being
4. associated with his person.
5. Why should others with cosmetics try to imitate his complexion
6. and steal the lifeless appearance of his vital color?
7. Why should inferior beauty seek to imitate
8. painted roses, when his rose of beauty is so natural?
9. Why should he live, now that naturalness is gone,
10. lacking blood to blush naturally?
11. For Nature has no reserves of natural beauty except in my love,
12. and Nature, proud of her great resources, lives solely upon his supply of beauty.
13. O, Nature keeps her reserves of beauty collected in him to show off her wealth
14. in days gone by, in contrast to the present imperfect times.

COMMENT: Here, as elsewhere, Shakespeare shows his dislike of the new fad for the use of cosmetics by women. As in the preceding sonnet he finds the times cheapened by those who trashily imitate genuine beauty. The poem is equally apt for our own days of television culture. Do not mistake the meaning of this sonnet—Shakespeare is not implying the use of cosmetics by his friend but his friend's concealing his sound natural beauty and morality under the veneer of an unsound and immoral way of life. The cosmetic sense is purely figurative, although Shakespeare indeed did detest the use of face paint.

(68)—"thus is his cheek . . ."

SUMMARY: *Nature uses my love's natural beauty as a guide to* *what beauty was like in the olden days—in contrast to the current corrupt cultivation of false beauty.*

PARAPHRASE

1. Thus is his face, like a map of outlived days,
2. when natural beauty lived and died as flowers do nowadays;
3. before substitutes for beauty were worn
4. or dared be put on a living face;
5. before the golden hair of the dead,
6. rightly belonging to the grave, was shorn away
7. to be used a second time on a second head—
8. in olden days beautiful hair from the dead was not used to make another gay.
9. In him those olden days are seen again,
10. without false ornament, natural and real,
11. not creating a false beauty for another,
12. nor robbing the old to renew his own loveliness.
13. And Nature preserves him as a guide
14. to show imitative art what beauty was like in the olden days.

COMMENT: Again, as in Sonnet 67, we see Shakespeare's preoccupation with false imitation whether in art or in cosmetics. An interesting custom to note here was the shearing of hair from corpses to be used for the newer and more elaborate wigs. Hubler correctly states that the ideal female beauty treasured her golden tresses, her lily-white skin, her rose-cheeks, and vermilion lips: "Ceruse, a popular cosmetic used to achieve whiteness, was a mixture of white lead and vinegar. Fucus, the strongest cosmetic used to produce the red, was made from red crystalline mercuric sulphide." (*Shakespeare's Songs and Sonnets,* p. 74). Note, for example, Hamlet's denunciation of Ophelia's (and womankind's) use of cosmetics and false ways, and see also Sonnet 67.

(69)—"those parts of thee . . ."

SUMMARY: *People praise your outward beauty but your deeds give them an evil impression of you; the truth is that you have cheapened yourself.*

PARAPHRASE

1. Your outward appearance viewed by the world
2. lacks nothing in the heart's imagination:

3. all true tongues pay you just due:
4. forced to admit the bare truth, even undenied by your foes.
5. Your outward appearance is thus crowned with outward praise,
6. but those same persons that give you your due in this manner,
7. destroy that praise of your outward appearance with other words
8. when they look beneath outward appearances and
9. see the beauty of your mind,
10. which they guess at by measuring your deeds;
11. then these boors, although seemingly praising you, mentally
12. connect your beauty with ugliness in deeds.
13.   But the reason your inner does not match your outer beauty
14.   lies here: that you have cheapened yourself with vulgar associations.

COMMENT: Beneath all of Shakespeare's paternal lecturing, we glimpse a touch of jealousy at his young friend's other associations; but whether with a Rival Poet, the Dark Lady or whatever, we do not know. The young friend has a deficiency of inner beauty as compared with his outward physical beauty. In previous sonnets the situation was reversed.

(70)—"that thou art blamed . . ."

SUMMARY: *Others envy your superb beauty, and if you remain without faults, you will be in charge of many devoted hearts.*

PARAPHRASE

1. That you are blamed (for having cheapened yourself) is not your fault,
2. for beauty is always the target of slander;
3. beauty is always regarded with suspicion,
4. like a crow flying through heavenly skies.
5. So long as you are good, slander only proves
6. your worth the greater, in spite of your being wooed by the temptations of our times;
7. for vice, like a flower cancer, prefers only the sweetest buds,
8. and your youthful beauty is pure and unsmirched.
9. You have passed through the dangers of youth,
10. either never tempted or victorious under attack;
11. yet my praise for you cannot be praise enough
12. to silence envy, which always grows in strength.
13.   If there were no suspicion of fault in your appearance,
14.   then you alone would be in command of whole kingdoms of hearts.

COMMENT: In Sonnet 69 the youth was inwardly flawed; here he is not. The explanation usually given is that the order of the 1609 Quarto, which is being followed here is corrupt (see Introduction). But O. J. Campbell finds this sonnet to logically follow 69. Reproach and forgiveness is a common theme in these sonnets, implied forgiveness here following hard upon the reproach of the preceding sonnet.

(71)—"no longer mourn..."

SUMMARY: *I should prefer your love for me to die when I die, lest the world see you grieving for me, and mock you because of me.*

PARAPHRASE

1. When I am dead mourn for me no longer
2. than the sound of the dark and gloomy bell,
3. which warns the world that I have fled
4. from this vile world to dwell with vile grave worms.
5. Nay, if you read this line of verse, do not recall to your mind
6. the poet who wrote it; for I love you so
7. that I should prefer your forgetting me,
8. if the remembrance should make you sorrowful.
9. O, if, I say, you should read this verse of mine,
10. when perhaps I shall have been blended with the clay from my grave,
11. do not so much as utter my name,
12. but rather let your love die even with my life
13.   lest the sophisticated world inquire into your grief,
14.   and mock you because of me after I am gone.

COMMENT: Sonnets 71 and 72 contain the same theme. They should be read together. The poet seems discouraged by lack of recognition as an artist and is also perhaps ashamed of his low professional caste as an actor. The mood is funereal and elegiac, resulting in one of the greatest poems in the language. Mark Van Doren called this sonnet, "one of the perfect English poems, though it is not among the mighty ones." As in all great elegies (*Lycidas, Adonais, Thyrsis*), the poet is actually mourning for himself. Some claim the sonnet is out of place and should follow 74, but the reader can determine this for himself.

Imagery: *The surely sullen bell* is a vivid image: bells tolling the funeral service are given human characteristics of surliness and sullenness, making the emotional impact unforgettable. The lack of imagery in the remaining lines implies the sincerity of direct utterance without embellishment and adds to the powerful statement of the theme. Here the couplet pictures the "wise world" (cultured contemporaries of the youth) mocking the youth along with Shakespeare's name.

Structure: The structure is flawless, and as in sonnet 64, the couplet is not tacked on to an already completed poem, but flows from, continues and completes the sense of the preceding quatrains. See also discussion of irony below.

Technique: Alliteration in *surly, sullen* (2) by the very sound of the sibilant s's gives the effect of muted grief and sorrow. The couplet achieves a vowel-*assonance* in the use of long o's and i's: *wise world, moan, me, gone*—adding to the sombre funereal effect. The *off-rhyme* (moan: gone) adds a twist of sad wryness, indicating an emotionally off-key mood.

Irony: This sonnet uses irony to undercut brilliantly the apparent meaning of the poem. Though it is perhaps "wise" to forget a loved one as soon as he is in the grave, it might be more desirable to be an object of mockery to such hollow sophisticates than to be so totally lacking in depth of feeling. What Shakespeare is really saying in this poem, then, is that he hopes his friend will not be "wise" but will mourn him when he is dead.

(72)—"o, lest the world . . ."

SUMMARY: *Lest your praise of me after I die seem false and bring shame upon you, forget me on my death; for I am ashamed of the quality of my verse—as you shall be.*

PARAPHRASE

1. O, lest the world challenge you to tell
2. what merit I had that you should go on loving me even
3. after my death, dear love, I beg you to forget me entirely;
4. for in me you will find nothing worthwhile,
5. unless you invent some false attribute of worth in me,
6. in order to do more for me than I deserve,
7. and render more praise to my dead corpse

8. than the miserable truth should allow.
9. O, lest your loyal love may seem false when you praise me;
10. when you, out of love for me, seem to give me false praise,
11. let my name be buried where my body lies;
12. so that I live no more to bring shame upon you or me.
13.   For I am ashamed of this verse I write,
14.   and so should you be, to love that which is worth nothing.

COMMENT: See Sonnet 71 to which this is a kind of inferior antiphon.

(73)—"that time of year . . ."

SUMMARY: *My feeling of near death-like sorrow when seen by you will make you cherish me more before you take your journey; or, my imminent death seen by you will make you love me more.*

PARAPHRASE

1. You may behold in me a feeling like that season of the year,
2. when few or no yellow leaves hang
3. upon boughs shaking in the cold air, like the
4. bare, ruined choirs of a cathedral, boughs on which birds lately were singing.
5. In me you may behold a feeling resembling the twilight
6. just after the sun has sunk in the west,
7. which twilight at once turns into a black night
8. resembling sleep (Death's second self), in that during night all is at rest.
9. In me you may behold a feeling resembling a glowing of embers
10. lying on a bed of dead ashes, which were formerly live coals, ashes now of the fire's once blazing youth,
11. resembling an ashy death-bed on which the glowing embers must soon expire,
12. consumed by the very ashes which formerly gave the fire vigorous life.
13.   Seeing this as my condition, increases your love for me
14.   and makes you cherish me more before you take yourself soon away from me (or makes you cherish me more before I die).

COMMENT: Hubler calls Sonnet 73 "a perfect instance of the Shakespearean sonnet." There is a pause following each quatrain, the longest pause coming after the third. Each quatrain treats one chief, visual image—autumn, twilight, a glowing fire almost dead—all uniting to create a solemn awareness of near-death:

> "The couplet, two adagio lines, comments on what has gone before without the slightest suggestion of the epigrammatic which so often mars the conclusion of Shakespeare's sonnets." (Hubler, p. 80.)

Rowse, p. 149, calls this sonnet "extremely beautiful and much admired:

> "Bare, ruined choirs' brings to the eye the roofless shells of monastic churches which stood out rawly to anyone traveling round England in the latter part of the sixteenth century; and 'where late the sweet birds sang' carries a characteristic double suggestion."

O. J. Campbell in his Bantam edition (p. 102) calls this sonnet "one of the most famous and most artfully composed of all the sonnets in the sequence."

Imagery: Quatrain 1: Shakespeare compares himself (in a metaphor) to autumn when trees are virtually bare of leaves. In an allied metaphor he compares the forest of bare *trees* to "bare ruined *choirs* where late the sweet birds sang." That is, the trees remind him of the Gothic outlines of ruined abbeys and monasteries; the *boughs* where lately the sweet *birds* sang then would by implication be the *choirstalls* and *choirsingers* which now are empty of their vocalists—a superb image and one of the greatest in English literature. In sum, the metaphors give us a minute and vivid picture of Shakespeare's desolate feelings. *Quatrain 2* shows Shakespeare comparing his condition to a *sunset,* just as the sun has sunk, at which point black night, *death's second self* (a secondary metaphor in which *night* is compared not to death but to death's best imitator, *sleep* and rest). So that is how Shakespeare feels—almost on the point of death. *Quatrain 3:* This contains the most difficult of the metaphors: Shakespeare compares himself to a glowing *bed of coals* almost on the point of dying out; the coals are lying on a bed of ashes which formerly had given great "nourishment" to the fire, but now are piled up high as dead ashes—enough to kill what few remaining living embers are left. This metaphoric statement is a profound analysis of the tragic condition of life, which dies the sooner, the more intensely it lives. That fire on the point of death is exactly how the poet himself feels. *Couplet:* The three metaphors point logically to their application in the couplet, which is not tacked on, but issues as a logical consequence of the three statements made in the three preceding quatrains. Shakespeare's friend now perceives this condition of near-death on Shakespeare's part, and, noticing Shakespeare's condition, will love Shakespeare much more knowing that the poet has not long to live. Some take line 14 in the sense that the friend should cherish the poet all the more, knowing that the friend is soon to absent himself. It is in both senses that I have written my paraphrase (see above, 14).

Technique: Shakespeare's technique is most subtle in metrical *variants:* the pause after *leaves, none, few* (2) adds an emotional effect of slow and tragic solemnity intensifying the mood. In *Bare ruined choirs* (4), three strong stresses vary the iambic pattern (the first metrical foot is a spondee, the second a trochee), give emphasis and weight to the meanings of those words; in addition the vowels, stretched out and lingering, in those three words, magically re-create the Gothic desolation by mood, sound, stress, and picture. The artful use of alliteration in *by and by black night* with their initial plosive consonants gives a stark effect of sheer horror. Especially subtle is the alliteration in line 8 where the sibilant s's slither and slide stealthily along while "death's second self . . . seals up all in rest."

(74)—"but be contented . . ."

SUMMARY: *When I die you will have lost merely the dregs of your lover's life—his body merely; but the body's spirit lives on in my verse which remains with you.*

PARAPHRASE

1. But be content; when fatal death
2. irretrievably shall carry me off,
3. my life will still have a share in this verse,
4. which will remain forever with you as a memorial.
5. When you read this verse, you are really seeing
6. the very part of myself which I consecrated to you:
7. the earth can receive earth (my body) only, its due;
8. but my spirit, the better part of me, is yours.
9. So then you have only lost my body, the dregs of life,
10. the prey of worms, my body being lifeless,
11. killed in a cowardly way by sneaking Time,

12. a body too base and unworthy for you to remember.
13.   The only worth of the body is the spirit it contains;
14.   and the spirit is here in my verse, which remains with you.

COMMENT: This sonnet completes a series on the poet's imagined death, which began in sonnet 71. It is a powerful statement arrayed in a vivid and simple metaphor; in some ways it is greater than the great Sonnet 73, just as Milton's *Paradise Regained,* in its more restrained style and less ambitious scope, is considered by some to be greater than *Paradise Lost.*

Imagery: Death is pictured as a *sheriff* who offers no *bail* (1-2), and in line 11, *it* is pictured as a *coward* wielding an evil knife, "The coward conquest of a wretch's knife"—a starkly terrible image.

(75)—"so are you to my thoughts . . ."

SUMMARY: *I alternately feast and starve for the sight of you, the sole source of my joy in life.*

PARAPHRASE

1. You are as vital to my thoughts as food is to life;
2. or as sweet spring showers which give vitality to earth;
3. to find content in you I struggle with my self
4. as a miser does with his riches:
5. now gloating over it, and then
6. fearing that thieving time will rob him of his wealth;
7. so do I now think it best to be alone with you, and
8. am then made happier by the world's seeing our friendship;
9. sometimes I feast my eyes full upon you, and
10. then later am starved for a glimpse of you:
11. I have none nor do I pursue any joy
12. except what I obtain from you.
13.   Thus do I alternately starve and glut my eyes upon you day after day,
14.   either having all of you or nothing at all.

COMMENT: In the keen competition for his patron's favor, Shakespeare here reveals his alternately hot and cold emotional state over the uncertainties of his place in his friend's heart and his pain upon their separations. A clever if ineffectual sonnet. "The filching age (6) is a good phrase.

(76)—"why is my verse so barren . . ."

SUMMARY: *I use old words in new ways to tell of my love, thus avoiding the latest fads in word usage.*

PARAPHRASE

1. Why is my verse so devoid of the latest fads,
2. containing neither variation nor lively changes?
3. Why do I not stay in tune with the latest modes, turn
4. to new techniques and oddly used words?
5. Why do I always write in the same manner,
6. keeping my imagination tuned to a familiar style,
7. so that every word almost reveals my name,
8. indicating they were uttered by me?
9. Then know, sweet love, I always write about you,
10. and you and love are always my theme:
11. so that the best I am capable of is the use of familiar words in a newer way,
12. employing themes already used by me before.
13. Just as the sun is every day new and old,
14. so is my verse of love always repeating what has already been told.

COMMENT: A very revealing sonnet. In addition to being a political conservative, Shakespeare, in his very use of the language maintained his conservatism, rejecting the poetic faddism popular among his colleagues. Important in this regard is line 7: "That every word doth almost tell my name". Shakespeare claims the distinctiveness of his style among the experimental products of his time. Very likely the new style is that of John Donne and the Metaphysical Poets. (See the Comment on Sonnet 24, a sonnet, by the way, which refutes Shakespeare's present assertion that he never writes contrived verse.)

(77)—"thy glass will show . . ."

SUMMARY: *Your mirror will remind you how time flies, and this book, if used properly, will enrich your mind, both the book and you profiting thereby.*

PARAPHRASE

1. Your mirror will reveal whether you are still beautiful,

2. and your pocket-dial will reveal how time flies;
3. the blank leaves of this book I give you will contain your jotted-down thoughts,
4. while from this book of verse (and blank leaves) you will learn this:
5. the wrinkles honestly seen in your mirror
6. will bring to your mind a picture of open graves;
7. the movement of your dial's secret stealthy shadow will teach you that
8. time stealthily and secretly moves towards eternity.
9. Look at this book and what you cannot remember
10. write in the blank pages; and you will find
11. that your thoughts, nursed like new-born children delivered from the mother-brain—
12. will make you newly acquainted with your own mind.
13.   These things—book and mirror—as often as glanced at,
14.   will profit both you and the book.

COMMENT: Notice the rather fatherly pedagogic tone here: Shakespeare is presenting a book filled with poems and blank pages in which his friend may both read and jot down his thoughts, thus encouraging him to compose and write. The image comparing *thoughts* to new-born *children* is still conventional, as in the popular phrase "brain child." This is an interesting *duty-sonnet*.

(78)—"so oft have I..."

SUMMARY: *Other poets write better poetry under your own patronage and inspiration, but you are the source of all my skill and serve to turn my ignorance into learning.*

PARAPHRASE

1. So often have I been inspired by you in my poetry,
2. and found such fine inspiration,
3. that other poets have taken up my habit,
4. and with you also as their inspiration, dispense poetry under your own patronage.
5. Your eyes, which taught the dumb in me to sing in exultation,
6. and my ignorance to turn into intelligence,
7. have inspired the poetry of my rivals to still higher strains,
8. and given their poetry a double intensity.
9. Yet be most proud of my verse,

10. which is under your influence and inspired by you.
11. In other poems by other poets you merely improve the style,
12. their art graced by your charm and nobility.
13.   But you are all my art, and serve to raise me
14.   from ignorance to learning.

COMMENT: Here Shakespeare again speaks of rival poets who seek his friend's patronage. Note the envy our poet shows of their learning, Shakespeare not being university trained as they most probably were, and the sweetly rationalized bit in the final couplet. Sonnets 78-86 deal with the same theme. The rival mentioned in 79, 80, 83, and 85 is known as the Rival Poet.

(79)—"whilst I alone . . ."

SUMMARY: *Your poet praises you but he can give you no praise that I have not already put there—nor need you thank him, since your beauty is eternal recompense for his words of praise.*

PARAPHRASE

1. While I alone called upon your aid,
2. only my verse was in your grace;
3. but now my gracious metrics are getting poorer in quality,
4. and my lame inspiration is being replaced by that of another poet.
5. I grant, sweet love, you, as a theme for poetry,
6. deserve the work of a worthier poet;
7. yet whatever your poet invents about you
8. is stolen from you in the first place, and then returned.
9. What he writes lends you virtue, but he stole his words
10. from your own virtuous character; he writes that he gives you beauty,
11. but he already found that quality in your cheek; he can give you
12. no words of praise, since that praise is always part of you;
13.   then thank that poet not for what he writes,
14.   since what he owes you, you are paying for yourself.

COMMENT: A natural continuation of Sonnet 78. But for the first time a specific "Rival Poet" is mentioned (see Introduction). The poem is ingenious but strained and insincere—and again the envy shows. The best candidates for the Rival Poet are Chapman and Marlowe, but the identity of that poet shall remain unknown unless new evidence is discovered.

(80)—"o, how I faint . . ."

SUMMARY: *The other poet obtains the height of your favor, but my verse, though inferior, still shares in it. If he thrives in your favor and I do not, then my love for you was the cause of my downfall.*

PARAPHRASE

1. O, how I faint when I now write about you,
2. knowing a better poet can use your name;
3. and in praising it spends all his energies,
4. so that I am tongue-tied when speaking of your fame.
5. But since your worth is as wide as the ocean,
6. which can bear both the humble and proud sail,
7. my impertinent craft, far inferior to the other poet's,
8. boldly appears in your circle.
9. Your slightest favor keeps me encouraged [afloat].
10. while the other poet rides upon the unfathomed depths of your favor;
11. But if I am wrecked by losing your favor, I can only conclude that my craft is worthless
12. while his remains mighty and proud.
13. Then if he thrives in your favor and I am cast away,
14. the worst was this: my love for you was the cause of my downfall.

COMMENT: See Sonnets 78 and 79 as preliminary. Here the Rival Poet seems to be basking in the favor of Shakespeare's friend or patron; and in addition his poetry seems superior, mightier, and prouder in its swing. Shakespeare's insecurity is quite evident. See Introduction on Rival Poet theories. Lines 5-12 contain an extended nautical conceit in which the friend is compared to the wide ocean, the poet to a "saucy bark" and "worthless boat" and the rival poet to "the proudest sail." Though a "humble" boat may venture upon the ocean, and may be kept more easily afloat in the shallow areas, its chances of survival in deeper areas are naturally less favorable than those of a larger, better built ship.

(81)—"or I shall live . . ."

SUMMARY: *My verse will keep your memory alive even for future generations.*

PARAPHRASE

1. Either I shall live to write your epitaph,
2. or else you will live when I am long dead;
3. death cannot take away your memory from my verse,
4. although I may be completely forgotten.
5. Your name from my verse shall obtain immortality;
6. though I, once dead, must be unknown to all the world:
7. for me the earth will yield but a forgotten grave,
8. while you will be remembered by all men after you die;
9. your monument will be found in my gentle verse,
10. which future generations yet unborn shall be reading;
11. and future generations shall be speaking of you,
12. when all those now living shall have perished:
13.   You will still live on—there is such power in my verse—
14.   where there is the most breath—in the mouths and tongues of mankind.

COMMENT: Shakespeare's legitimate pride in the immortalizing power of his verse is well expressed here; there is even a strong affirmation that his own reputation will endure—as it most assuredly did.

(82)—"I grant thou wert . . ."

SUMMARY: *You accept the praise of other poets, but their strained rhetoric does not rival my sympathetic and honest poems: their verse of praise might be better directed elsewhere than by superfluously sending it to you.*

PARAPHRASE

1. I admit that you were not dedicated to my poetry alone,
2. and therefore you may without fault peruse
3. the words of devotion in dedications to you by other poets,
4. who beg their lovely subject to favor all their books.
5. You are as wide in knowledge as you are lovely in looks;
6. and knowing your worth to extend beyond and above my praise,
7. you are therefore forced to seek again
8. some fresher poetry in these improving times.
9. And please do so, my love; yet when they have dreamed up
10. lines containing exaggerated strains of rhetoric,
11. your true goodness would be more truthfully represented

12. in plain words of truth by your truth-telling friend.
13.   And their colored praise in verse might be better used
14.   for paler patrons—such verse as theirs is a misuse.

COMMENT: We learn more of the kind of verse written by the rival poets: it is strained, exaggerated, and rhetorical. Most of the biography-reading critics suggest Chapman, Jonson, or Marlowe as likely candidates. Speculation is useless since there is no confirming evidence yet available. Certainly the rivals were intellectuals (Spenser, Marlowe, Greene, Nashe, Sidney, Lyly, Peele, Lodge were all university wits, whereas Shakespeare had but a grammar school education). Shakespeare looked upon himself neither as intellectual nor progressive: he was backward-looking and nostalgic in his views, say the best historical critics, and certainly the sonnets bear him out.

(83)—"I never saw . . ."

SUMMARY: *You blame me for my silence in poetry, but I was silent in the face of your indescribable beauty. Other poets praise you and fail, since there is more life in one of your eyes than both your poets can find power enough to invent praise for.*

PARAPHRASE

1. I never saw that your beauty needed cosmetic enhancement,
2. and therefore your beauty did I not enhance in verse;
3. I found, or thought I found, you did not need
4. the worthless offering of a poet's verse in payment;
5. and therefore I have been lax in your praise,
6. since you yourself, living, well might show
7. how far a modern poet falls short
8. in praise of your worth, which itself grows in you.
9. My silence in verse was called sinful by you,
10. but it in fact was most glorious, keeping silent
12. when other poets would offer you immortality and fail.
13.   There is more life in one of your fair eyes
14.   than both your poets can invent in their verse.

COMMENT: "Both your poets" (14) refers to Shakespeare and his rival for the patronage of the friend, the so-called "Rival Poet" (see Introduction). Line 4 "The barren tender of a poet's debt" shows his fondness for imagery of the bank-

ing house: the *poet* dedicating his poetry to a patron is compared to a *person* repaying a debt which is worthless in value.

(84)

SUMMARY: *Let poets but copy your beauty in verse, not try to praise you—and they shall be famous for their power to create images of beauty.*

PARAPHRASE

1. Whoever says most in praise of you, can say no
2. more than this rich praise: you alone are your self,
3. in whose person is contained all the qualities
4. necessary to create an example equal to you.
5. That poet is a poor one,
6. who does not lend some small glory to his subject;
7. but he that writes of you
8. that you are your self, gives dignity to his work.
9. Let him but copy what is written in you,
10. and not make worse what nature made so clear;
11. and such copying shall make the poet famous for wit,
12. making his style admired everywhere.
13. You to your beauteous blessings add a curse,
14. since you are fond of the praise of others, and their praise can never be adequate to your worth.

COMMENT: A duty-sonnet on the subject of the rival poet or poets. The Quarto reading for line 1 puts a question mark after *most*.

(85)—"my tongue-tied muse..."

SUMMARY: *I cannot write praise of you as others do in golden words. My love is silent in my thoughts and speaks best in that way.*

PARAPHRASE

1. My poetry, out of politeness, remains silent,
2. while other poets praise you, in rich terms,
3. preserving their writing in golden words,
4. and in precious phrases artfully laid out.
5. I think good thoughts, while other poets write fine words;

6. and, like an illiterate cleric, I still approve
7. every poem of praise rendered by able poets
8. in polished form and in a highly refined style.
9. Hearing you praised, I say "It's true, it's true,"
10. and to the highest praise I add something else—
11. but that praise is in my thoughts, where my love
12. for you comes before words.
13.   Then respect other poets for the breath they expend in words,
14.   but respect me for my silent thoughts of love forcefully presenting my case.

COMMENT: A duty-sonnet, conventionally clever, but it may be a clever alibi to cover up a period of laziness on our poet's part. He has not written poems to the number and in the time he should have. This is the last sonnet to deal in the present tense with the famous Rival Poet; and here Shakespeare admits (as elsewhere) the superiority of the other poet, of which superiority I am sure he was not by any means convinced.

(86)—"was it the proud full sail . . ."

SUMMARY: *It was not the mighty verse of my rival which has silenced me but your favoring his verse which has left me tongue-tied and uninspired.*

PARAPHRASE

1. Was it the proud, mighty words of that poet's great verse
2. written to win your precious favor
3. that sealed my ripe thoughts inside my brain,
4. making the brain the place where my thoughts both originated and died?
5. Was it his spirit that was taught by invisible divine spirits to write
6. verse of heavenly power, which left me speechless?
7. No, neither he nor his night-companions,
8. giving him aid, could stun my verse into silence.
9. Neither he, nor that affable friendly ghost,
10. which nightly tricks him with secret information,
11. can boast they cowed me into silence.
12. I was not sick with fear of them;
13.   but when you approved his verse,
14.   then I lacked inspiration: that is what has enfeebled mine.

COMMENT: Rowse calls the eighty-sixth sonnet the most important autobiographically. He explains that the rival is written of in the *past* tense, indicating the rivalry now past. The year must be 1593, the very year Marlowe was killed at Deptford on May 30. Marlowe dabbled with spirits, played with atheism in *Dr. Faustus* (this can explain lines 9-10), and Marlowe had just before gained in the patron's (i.e., the Earl of Southampton's) favor. Hubler calls all such speculation idle since the evidence is flimsy. Many critics call Chapman the rival poet, since his style also was of the proud and mighty type (see Introduction).

Imagery: The "proud full sail" of line 1 refers back to the nautical conceit of Sonnet 80.

(87)—"farewell: thou art too dear . . ."

SUMMARY: *You have taken back your love for me, since it was based on an overestimation, and that has left me desolate.*

PARAPHRASE

1. Farewell! you are too precious for me to possess you,
2. and likely enough you know your own worth;
3. your essential worth releases you from any claim of mine;
4. and my hold on you is at an end.
5. Nor can I have a hold on you but by your wish;
6. and how do I deserve such a reward?
7. The justification in me for such a fine gift is lacking,
8. and so my right to you is negated.
9. Your self you gave to me, not realizing then your own worth;
10. or else you overestimated me, to whom you gave your self;
11. so the great gift of your love, given in an overestimation,
12. is withdrawn now that you have arrived at better judgment.
13.   Thus I have had your love, like a flattering dream;
14.   in sleep, when dreaming of your love for me, I was a king, but upon awakening it was no such matter.

COMMENT: In this tragic sonnet of farewell, part of the series dealing with the Rival Poet, Shakespeare takes his leave of his love, accepting the fact that he has been rejected.

Technique: Note that except for lines 2 and 4, the line endings are all feminine, giving the poem a note of trailing and falling farewell, a delicate touch indeed. In lines 2 and 4 the meaning and rhythm are uniquely handled.

Imagery: The metaphors are from the business field again, but here done so fittingly that there is no clash between sentiment and image: *possessing, estimate, releasing, charter, bonds, determinate, patent, worth* etc. In the comparison in line two, for example, the friend's *virtue* is compared to a *charter* on which Shakespeare has a lien.

(88)—"when thou shalt be . . ."

SUMMARY: *When you shall want to get rid of me, I will defend your action, and to justify you I will bear all insults and injuries.*

PARAPHRASE

1. Whenever you are disposed to regard me lightly,
2. and look with scorn on my worth,
3. I will be on your side, in opposition to my own true feelings;
4. and prove you are virtuous, although you are a betrayer.
5. Since I am best aware of my own weakness,
6. in your interest I can relate a story
7. of concealed faults, of which I am guilty;
8. but in getting rid of me you shall be the gainer too:
9. and I by losing you will a gainer too;
10. for in turning all my loving thoughts upon you,
11. the injuries that I do to myself
12. will be of double value to me by doing you good.
13.   Such is my love, and to you I belong so much
14.   that to justify you, I shall bear all insults.

COMMENT: Note particularly line 4, in which Shakespeare utters his most bitter criticism, not too well concealed beneath his surface humility and protestations of love. This sonnet continues the series dealing with the poet's rejection by the friend.

(89)—"say that thou didst . . ."

SUMMARY: *Your forsaking me will make me hate myself—since I can never love him whom you hate.*

PARAPHRASE

1. Say that you forsook me for some fault of mine,
2. and I will comment upon that fault;
3. Speak of my lameness, and immediately will I be lame,
4. making no defence against your charges.
5. You cannot, love, disgrace me half so badly as
6. to make your rejection of me look respectable,
7. I shall disgrace myself; knowing your desire,
8. I will deny our acquaintance and act like a stranger;
9. I keep away from places you frequent; and I will speak
10. your sweet beloved name no more,
11. lest I, being so profane, should disgrace your name and do it wrong
12. and by chance tell others of our friendship.
13.   Against my self I swear to debate for your sake,
14.   for I must never love him whom you hate.

COMMENT: See Comment to Sonnet 88.

(90)—"then hate me . . ."

SUMMARY: *Your abandonment of me should be done at the onset of my woes; for then other griefs by comparison will not seem so great.*

PARAPHRASE

1. Then hate me whenever you wish; if at any time, then now is the best time;
2. now, while the world is determined to frustrate my actions,
3. join with bad luck and, together, crush me;
4. and do not add to that by heaping woes on me later.
5. Ah, do not, when I shall have recovered from this sorrow,
6. follow it up with another woe,
7. like a rainy day after a windy night,
8. in order to prolong my planned overthrow.
9. If you wish to leave me, do not be the last to do so,
10. just when other petty griefs have done their worst;
11. but come at the beginning of my disgrace: thus I shall taste,
12. at the very beginning, the worst bitterness and power of fate.
13.   Then other griefs, which now seem tragic,
14.   compared with my loss of you will no longer seem so.

COMMENT: This is a follow-up to the preceding sonnet.

Rowse believes that this was a bitter period for our poet, who was out of work during the plague years in 1592 and 1593. But this is speculation, since no one can date the sonnets exactly, and no one can determine what depressed Shakespeare at this juncture. Injured love is now expressed in a much less ornamented style than in the earlier sonnets.

(91)—"some glory in their birth..."

SUMMARY: *To me your love is the sum of all joys, and I am wretched only in the thought that you may take your love from me.*

PARAPHRASE

1. Some people glory in their birth, some in their artistry,
2. some in their wealth, some in their body's strength;
3. some in their clothes, even though new-fangled and unattractive;
4. some in their hawks and hounds, some in their horses.
5. Each disposition has its own corresponding joy
6. when even the least of misfortunes, my life, would end if I
7. but these individual pleasures do not fit my standard of happiness.
8. I outdo all these pleasures in one overall best joy:
9. your love is better to me than nobility,
10. richer than wealth, prouder than the cost of clothes;
11. of more delight than hawks or horses;
12. and having you, I boast more proudly than all the others.
13.   I am wretched in this thought alone, that you may take
14.   all this pleasure away from me and render me most wretched.

COMMENT: The bitter tensions of Sonnet 90 are here lessened, but note the couplet that reminds us of the old tragedy. It would appear that the relationship of poet and friend was not always sycophantic, as some suggest.

(92)—"but do thy worst..."

SUMMARY: *My life is completely dependent upon your love.*

PARAPHRASE

1. Though you may do your worst to steal yourself away from me,
2. you are still mine during my lifetime;

3. and my life will last no longer than your love for me,
4. for my life is dependent wholly upon your love.
5. Then I need not fear the worst of misfortunes,
6. when even the least of misfortunes, my life would end if I had not your love.
7. A better life awaits me than that
8. which depends upon your moods.
9. You can not trouble me with your inconstancy,
10. since my life would end if you turned away from me.
11. O, what a joyous right I have:
12. happy for your love, and happy to die upon its loss!
13. But what is so beautiful and good that one need not fear a flaw?
14. You may be false, and yet I might not be aware of it.

COMMENT: Shakespeare is still in a state of jealous depression here, but more significant is the rebuke at the end. Sonnets 93-96 continue this strain of rebuke.

(93)—"so shall I live..."

SUMMARY: *Your looks permanently indicate sweet love. There is in them no indication of a change of heart, but if your goodness matched not your outward appearance, your beauty would be like the apple of Eve.*

PARAPHRASE

1. So I shall continue to live in your love, supposing you true to me,
2. like a deceived husband; so even the appearance of love
3. may still seem true to me, though it really has been recently changed.
4. You direct an appearance of love towards me, but your heart is elsewhere.
5. Your eye is incapable of hatred;
6. and therefore by looking into your eyes I should not know your love has changed:
7. in the looks of many the false lover is betrayed
8. by his moodiness, frowning, and altered features.
9. But heaven, while creating you, had decreed
10. that sweet love should dwell permanently in your looks;
11. whatever the thoughts in your brain or feelings of your heart may be,

12. your looks would reveal nothing except your own sweetness.
13. How like Eve's apple are your beautiful looks,
14. if their sweetness is not expressive of true virtue.

COMMENT: Except for some bare similes, our poet sticks to the plain tongue and direct statement, indicating a maturity of style and greater intensity of vision. A besetting theme occurring often in the plays now begins to appear in the sonnets: the difference between appearance and reality. The lover's countenance shows only love for Shakespeare, but what are the true feelings within his breast? This question continues to torture Shakespeare with jealousy.

(94)—"they that have pow'r . . ."

SUMMARY: *They are the inheritors of heaven's graces and nature's riches, preserving them for mankind, who do not use their gifts unjustly; but if you use your beauty to hurt others, your loss of inner virtue will corrupt your appearance.*

PARAPHRASE

1. Those who have power to hurt others and yet will not do so;
2. who do not do that which their appearance most indicates;
3. who, stirring others to love, are like stone themselves—
4. unmoved, coldhearted, and not easily tempted;
5. such people quite justly inherit heaven's graces and charms,
6. and preserve in themselves the riches of nature from going to waste;
7. they are in complete command of their excellent revealed qualities,
8. where others are but custodians of them.
9. The summer's flower adds a sweet fragrance to summertime,
10. even though it lives and dies for itself only;
11. but if that flower should become internally diseased,
12. the ugliest weed would surpass it in beauty.
13. For the loveliest things turn bad through their actions;
14. Lilies that turn rotten smell far worse than weeds.

COMMENT: A powerful poem on the discrepancy between the superficial appearance of beauty and its true nature. Those men whose appearance does not match their deeds are not the true inheritors of heaven's graces. Again we see the parable of the talents (Matthew 25: 14-30): man is Nature's *steeped in sin.*

steward and her gifts must be put to good use. The sestet states the theme correctly. Be it observed that the concern has changed from the mere physical beauty of the earlier sonnets to moral beauty.

(95)—"how sweet and lovely..."

SUMMARY: *Your sexual sins are staining your virtuous reputation through evil gossip. The sins, because of your beauty, look lovely, but take care; for even the loveliest virtue turns ugly when steeped in sin.*

PARAPHRASE

1. How fetchingly lovely do you make your shameful actions,
2. which, like a worm in a rose,
3. stain the virtuous goodness of your budding reputation!
4. O, in what a lovely body are your shameful deeds contained!
5. Those persons who relate how you spend your days,
6. making bawdy remarks about your sexual love affairs,
7. can not dispraise you; but they do render you a kind of false praise;
8. just mentioning your name serves to bless their evil remarks.
9. O, in what a fair person are those vices found,
10. which chose you as their home;
11. where your beauty conceals their ugliness,
12. and gives ugly sins a lovely appearance to be seen by all.
13.   Take care, dear love, of the wide liberty you enjoy:
14.   the hardest and sharpest knife, badly used, loses its edge.

COMMENT: Again the theme of the discrepancy between inward and outward beauty, a commonplace in sixteenth century poetry.

Imagery: "The hardest knife ill-used doth lose his edge" is a great line in its simplicity and popular proverbial character —where Shakespeare is at his best.

(96)—"some say thy fault..."

SUMMARY: *Your faults are turned into graces through your beauty; but do not practice hypocrisy by concealing sins with your beauteous exterior. Since you are mine, however, you need not worry for my good estimate of you will insure your reputation.*

PARAPHRASE

1. Some say that your youthfulness is at fault; some say your sexual promiscuity;
2. others say that youthfulness and promiscuity are graces when found in you;
3. but both your graces and your faults are loved alike by both great and little people,
4. since you can convert your faults into living graces.
5. Just as on the finger of a queen
6. the cheapest jewel will be highly prized,
7. so similarly, the faults seen in you
8. are transformed into truths, and considered as truths by others.
9. Look how many innocent lambs the wolf might seize
10. if he could change his appearance into that of a lamb.
11. Look how many admirers you could lead astray
12. if you were to exert the full force of your beauty and nobility.
13.   But do not do this. I love you so much
14.   that since you are my love, my estimate of your reputation is that good reputation itself.

COMMENT: Queen Elizabeth was fond of jeweled rings. The concluding couplet repeats the ending of Sonnet 36. Such a repetition indicates Shakespeare probably had no hand in the Quarto arrangement of his poems. This sonnet closes the series begun with 92.

(97)—"how like a winter..."

SUMMARY: *I am desolate away from you, and the world shares my desolation.*

PARAPHRASE

1. Absence from you is to me like winter,
2. for you are like the pleasant summer in a fleeting year!
3. How I froze away from you, how dark the days!
4. The bare December landscape around me everywhere!
5. And yet the time of our parting was summertime;
6. The fruitful autumn season, loaded with harvest,
7. yields crops fertilized in the spring—
8. like children born of widows whose husbands have died:
9. Yet this fruitful harvest seemed to me
10. like orphans—without fathers;

11. for summer and its joys are dependent upon you,
12. and when you are absent, the very birds are silent;
13. or if they do sing, it is done so apathetically,
14. that even the summer leaves turn pale with grief at your absence, as if dreading the approach of winter.

COMMENT: The meaning of this difficult but unforgettable sonnet is clear if line 5 is understood. Though they had parted in summer and it is now only early autumn, Shakespeare feels as desolate away from his friend as if it were winter. This feeling affects his perception (known in critical terms as "the Pathetic Fallacy"). In *Quatrain 2, autumn* is compared to a pregnant *woman* big with child, having been made pregnant by the *prime* (early summer, line 7); but now the crops (autumn's children) seem like unfathered orphans since their father, summer, is now gone, just as Shakespeare, himself, feels desolated by the absence of his friend who brings summer into his life. This psychological state so influences his perception that it appears to him that even the birds and leaves reflect his feelings.

(98)—"from you have I..."

SUMMARY: *Absence from you in the spring leaves me sad, in spite of the gayety of the season; for the flowers (copies of you) brought you to my mind: but it seemed winter still as I played with these images of you.*

PARAPHRASE

1. In the springtime I was absent from you,
2. when gloriously colored April in all its beauty,
3. had put such a spirit of youth in all things,
4. that the heavy and sad planet Saturn himself laughed and leaped with the season.
5. Yet, neither the songs of birds, nor the sweet fragrance
6. of the various colored flowers,
7. could make me tell some joyful tale of summer,
8. or pick the flowers from the glorious earth where they grew:
9. nor did I admire the whiteness of the lily
10. or praise the deep vermilion of the rose;
11. since they were merely delightful forms
12. copied after you, their pattern.

13.　　Yet in spite of the season it still seemed winter to me, and with you away

14.　　I played with the flowers as if playing with your image.

COMMENT: Oscar J. Campbell calls 97 and 98 "two of the most beautiful poems in the entire sequence." In both sonnets, the friend's absence turns spring and summer into winter for the poet. Sonnet 97 is, however, incomparably finer.

(99)—"the forward violet . . ."

SUMMARY: *I noticed that all the lovely flowers had stolen their fragrances and colors directly from you.*

PARAPHRASE

1. Thus did I scold the early-appearing violet:
2. Sweet thief, from which place did you steal your fragrance,
3. if not from the breath of my friend? The proud red adornment
4. of your petals, like the color on a soft cheek, has been
5. too obviously colored in imitation of the blood in the veins of my love.
6. I condemned the lily for stealing the whiteness of your hand;
7. and the buds of marjoran for stealing your hair;
8. I condemned the roses which like fearful girls made themselves unpluckable because of their thorns:
9. the red rose blushing as if in shame, and the white blanching as if in despair;
10. I rejected a third, neither red nor white, because it had stolen its mingled color from the other two roses;
11. and to his theft he had added the perfume stolen from your breath;
12. but, because of his robbery, when he is in full blossom—
13. Let a vengeful worm eat him up and destroy him so that he perishes!
14. I noted more flowers, but all
15. had stolen their fragrance and color from you.

COMMENT: This is a rare sonnet in that it has 15 lines, the first five lines rhyming ababa. It is a poem rich in conceits which succeed in all their charming, sweet, and clever artifice, though lines 3-5 are somewhat obscure. *Purple* (line 3) generally means *red* in Elizabethan poetry. The word *eat* (Quarto reading), line 13, is *not* in the imperfect tense as Hubler would have it (p. 108); the sense requires a curse in the present.

(100)—"where art thou, muse . . ."

SUMMARY: *I lack inspiration to dedicate poetry to my love, but if time begins to age him, I shall pen satires against time's ravages.*

PARAPHRASE

1. Where are you, my goddess of inspiration, that you have forgotten so long
2. to speak of that which gives you all your power?
3. Do you expend your inspired ecstasy on some worthless poem,
4. diminishing your powers by glorifying unworthy subjects?
5. Return, forgetful goddess, and immediately redeem
6. in noble verses the time you have so idly spent on unworthy things;
7. recite to the ear of one who values your poems
8. and gives your poetry both skill and themes.
9. Rise, sluggish goddess, and look at the sweet face of my love;
10. if time has engraved any wrinkle there—
11. if there be any at all—then inspire me with the power to write satiric poetry against time's decay,
12. and make time's plunder despised everywhere.
13.   Give my love fame faster than time can decay life;
14.   in this way you can prevent the complete destructiveness of time.

COMMENT: The "fury" (3) is the same as the "fine frenzy" of *A Midsummer Night's Dream* (V,I,12). This may be a duty-sonnet but it makes pleasant reading. Sonnets 100-108 are optimistic and cheerful poems: Sonnet 107 will tell us why the poet is so glad.

There were nine muses among the Greek gods of Olympus, the function of the muse of poetry being to inspire poets to write stirring poems. Shakespeare's muse evidently had been lagging, but she certainly has succeeded in inspiring the poet to write immortally against time's decay (11-14).

(101)—"o truant muse . . ."

SUMMARY: *Do not excuse your long silence in neglecting to inspire me to write verse, O Muse of poetry, in praise of my love,* *by saying beauty needs no praise, since my love requires praise for his beauty to endure beyond the grave.*

PARAPHRASE

1. O irregularly present power of divine inspiration, what will you do to make up
2. for your neglect of inseparable truth and beauty?
3. Both truth and beauty are dependent upon my love,
4. and so are you, my goddess Muse, dependent upon my love, and are the nobler for it.
5. Give me an answer, my inspiring goddess: will you not perhaps say,
6. "Truth needs no decoration, since truth has its own beauty;
7. beauty needs not a poem to apply its truth to paper;
8. but each, beauty and truth, is best when not mixed with anything else"?
9. Because my love, like truth and beauty, needs no praise, should you, my inspiring goddess, be silent?
10. Do not use that argument as an excuse for lack of inspiration, for it is up to you, inspiring power,
11. to make my love endure beyond the grave,
12. and be praised by future generations.
13.   Then do your duty, divine goddess: I shall teach
14.   you how to make him seem truly beautiful in the eyes of future generations, just as he is now.

> **COMMENT:** *Truth* = value = worth = genuineness, in this sonnet. The opposite of true beauty is artificiality. Like Keats in his *Ode to a Grecian Urn*, Shakespeare finds truth and beauty inseparable in his friend (see Hubler edition of the Sonnets). I can't help feeling that there is here a lame excuse for Shakespeare's neglecting to write often enough to his friend hidden somewhere in this poem and others like it.

(102)—"my love is strength'ned in..."

SUMMARY: *My silence in writing more love poems to you is due to my fear that they shall be cheapened by becoming too often heard—and bore you.*

PARAPHRASE

1. My love is really stronger, although it seems weaker;

2. I do not love you less, though my praise appears less often in verse.
3. That love is cheapened when its high worth
4. is broadcast by the lover everywhere.
5. Our love was fresh and new in its inception,
6. when I used to celebrate it with my verse.
7. The nightingale sings early in summer
8. and stops in late summer;
9. not that she stops because late summer is less pleasant
10. than when her mournful songs hushed the night,
11. but that wild songs are heard on every bough,
12. and when good things become too common, they lose their appeal.
13. Therefore, like the nightingale, I sometimes write no poems of praise
14. because I do not wish to bore you with my poetry.

COMMENT: A lovely poem with the genuine freshness of a spring song.

Imagery: In the Greek myth Philomel, a maiden, was turned into a nightingale, in which form she continued to sing her tragic story. Incidentally, female nightingales do not sing, nor do the males cease singing for the reason here given.

Lovely Lines: "And stops his pipe in growth of riper days" (8).
 "And sweets grown common lose their dear delight" (12).

(103)—"alack, what poverty..."

SUMMARY: *Do not blame me for my silence in poetry of praise to you, but beauty needs no decoration.*

PARAPHRASE

1. Alas, my poems have been inferior products,
2. Although I have free play to show my powers;
3. for you as a subject, without poetic praise, are of more worth
4. than when my praise is added to your essential beauty.
5. O, do not blame me; I can write no more love poems!
6. Look in your mirror, and there will appear a face
7. that quite surpasses in beauty my poor poetic powers to praise;
8. and such poetry would do me little good.

9. Would it not be wrong then that in striving to improve something,
10. one can mar the subject that before was beautiful?
11. For my verses are written for no other reason
12. but to tell of your gifts and graces.
13.   And more beauty, much more,
14.   can be seen in your mirror when you gaze into it than can be seen in my verses of praise.

COMMENT: Shakespeare is repeating some of his themes here; see examples, Sonnet 77 and 101.

(104)—"to me, fair friend . . ."

SUMMARY: *To me your beauty will never grow old, but my eyes may be deceived—and before the future generations arrive, your beauty may be gone and forgotten.*

PARAPHRASE

1. To me, beautiful friend, you never can be old,
2. for as you were when first I saw you,
3. such seems your beauty still; three cold winters,
4. stripping the trees of their glorious leaves;
5. three beautiful springs, turning to yellow-colored autumn,
6. have I seen in the seasonal procession;
7. the sweet fragrances of three Aprils have been burned in three hot Junes
8. since I first saw you—who are still youthful.
9. Ah, yet beauty, like the shadow on a sun-dial,
10. steals away from its possessor unperceived—
11. and this is true of your youthful complexion, to my eyes ever youthful,
12. which nevertheless ages, making my eyes mistaken.
13.   So, for fear of this loss of youth, hear this, you ages of the future:
14.   beauty's perfection was gone before you arrived.

COMMENT: This *dating sonnet* indicates that Shakespeare wrote it three years after he had first seen his young friend. Rowse dates the three years from 1591-1594, p. 215. If the friend were the Earl of Southampton, he would have been eighteen in 1591, Shakespeare twenty-seven. The outrageous pun in line 2 ("when first your eye I eyed") is a tour-de-force in punning, the favorite game of Elizabethans, and, for that matter, one of the chief staples of many a humorist today. Let's look at "eye I eyed"; 1. When first your eye I ayed (When I first saw you I said "Aye"). 2. When first your aye I eyed (When I first saw you I saw your aye of agreement). 3. When first your aye I ayed, or I ayed, etc., etc.

(105)—"let not my love . . ."

SUMMARY: *I write only and ever to you and on one theme: your beauty, kindness and truth which never till now have been together in one person.*

PARAPHRASE

1. Do not let my love for you be called idolatry,
2. nor let my beloved appear as an idol,
3. since my poems of praise are written, all of them,
4. to one person, about one person, ever the same one, still the same one.
5. My love is kind today and will be so tomorrow,
6. and always constant in his wonderful excellence.
7. Therefore my verse is the soul of constancy,
8. expressing one thing only, omitting all variations.
9. My entire theme is, "Fair, kind, and true";
10. and "Fair, kind, and true" again in other words;
11. and all my invention is spent in varying this one theme,
12. which really is three themes in one, affording me wide range.
13.   "Fair, kind, and true," have lived apart,
14.   but not until now have the three been found in one person—my beloved.

   COMMENT: A duty-sonnet. *Kind = natural = benevolent = tender.*

(106)—"when in the chronicle . . ."

SUMMARY: *Olden-time stories in their praise of beauty merely prophesy yours, which we in this age lack skill enough to praise.*

PARAPHRASE

1. When in stories written in olden times
2. I see descriptions of the fairest persons,

3. and the old time verse made beautiful
4. in its praise of dead ladies and lovely knights;
5. then in the display of the most beautiful,
6. the hand, the foot, the lip, the eye, the brow,
7. I see that the old-time writers were trying to express
8. the very beauty that is yours now.
9. So all the praises to beauty of the old-time stories are but a foretelling to
10. this present day of your own beauty;
11. and because they looked only with prophetic eyes upon beauty,
12. they had not enough skill to celebrate your true worth.
13.   But we, in this present time,
14.   may look with amazement at your beauty, but lack the skill to give it adequate praise.

COMMENT: One likes to think that Shakespeare was reading that wonderful romance, Chaucer's "Knight's Tale." The muse of poetry has inspired Shakespeare here to write one of the greatest of his sonnets. Sonnet 103 is important here (which see) because there he discusses his inadequacy as an artist to the subject he was considering. Here too he expresses this same feeling of inadequacy (14) yet in the poem itself he has succeeded magnificently.

Structure: *Quatrain* 1 tells us about Shakespeare's reading in old chronicles about beauty; in *Quatrain* 2 he realizes that the old-time anonymous authors were trying to describe beauty, but in Quatrain 3, that they were merely foretelling the future beauty of his friend, and they were inadequately equipped, in subject matter, to describe the essence of all beauty as revealed in his friend. The word *still* (12) is often changed to *skill* by certain editors, but the meaning is "that the poets of olden times lacked the subject matter." (Hubler, p. 114).

The *Couplet:* As for the poets of the present day, they have the subject matter—the perfectly beautiful youth—but they lack the *skill* to describe him. The writers of olden times had the *skill* but *not* the subject matter. In the first three quatrains, the problem of describing beauty is given, while in the couplet, the paradoxical resolution is given, the inadequacy of modern poets to describe the foretold beauty of the youth.

Imagery: Line 3 shows that the subject matter (beauty) actually makes the old rhymes beautiful. Other than that image, there is little imagery, the direct and simple statement giving a flavor of olden times, its simplicity and quaint beauty, the style brilliantly suited to his beautiful subject matter.

Alden in his edition of the Sonnets says that the conceit undergoes a perfect development "in which every line is true to the controlling image, and the couplet perfectly completes its evolution" (Rollins' *Variorum*, I).

Great line: "And beauty making beautiful old rhyme" said by Alden to be the loveliest line of all in the entire sequence.

(107)—"not mine own fears . . ."

SUMMARY: *All is peace and certainty now, and my love looks youthful—and in my verse both he and I shall be made immortal.*

PARAPHRASE

1. Neither my own fears nor the prophetic soul
2. of the whole world speculating on future events,
3. can exert control over the fate of my beloved,
4. who is supposed to be subject to time and death.
5. The moon itself has survived its eclipse,
6. and the prophets who predicted woe after the eclipse are mocked by their own words;
7. former uncertainties have now triumphed as certainties,
8. and the peace we enjoy now promises to be eternal.
9. Now in this most prosperous of times,
10. my love looks fresh and youthful, and death does my will
11. since, in spite of death, I shall be made immortal in my poor verse,
12. while death lords it over less articulate writers.
13. And you will find your true monument in my verse,
14. even after tyrants and brass tombs have rotted away.

COMMENT: Hubler's comment is apt: the references in the second quatrain have led many scholars to attempt dating this sonnet, but they "have succeeded only in documenting their own predispositions." (Sonnets p. 116). A sampling should suffice:

O. J. Campbell: Shakespeare, out of danger from complicity in the Essex rebellion, rusticated with Pembroke in Wilton, suggesting a date of 1601, p. 136, Bantam edition, 1964.

A. L. Rowse: The Lopez conspiracy and the Peace of Paris suggests 1594 (see Rowse, Harper edition, p. 224).

Great line: "Peace proclaims olives of endless age."

See also important essay on 107 by; Leslie Hotson, *Shakespeare's Sonnets Dated* (1949) and F. W. Bateson's answer to it in *Essays in Criticism,* I (1951).

(108)—"what's in the brain . . ."

SUMMARY: *Finding nothing new to say about you I repeat myself ritually about my love for you, but do not consider it to be old. So eternal love disregards age and wrinkles because it endures beyond outward appearances.*

PARAPHRASE

1. What is there in my thoughts that may be written down
2. which I have not revealed to you, my true soul?
3. What new way can there be
4. to express my love or your cherished worth?
5. None, lovely boy; but yet like prayers at church service,
6. I must each day repeat myself,
7. finding old things not old, since you are mine, I yours;
8. even as at the time when I first made your name sacred to me.
9. So that a truly eternal love is always new,
10. and disregards the injuries of old age;
11. nor does it give way to the wrinkles of age;
12. but rather, eternal love makes old age its servant,
13.   finding in old age the first impressions of love born true;
14.   whereas time and outward features would suppose it dead.

COMMENT: A duty-sonnet, but interesting in that our poet admits to repetitiousness and, perhaps, a lagging inspiration. Again we have that old fear of wrinkles, an almost unnatural preoccupation, but for the fact that middle-aged gentlemen are generally wrinkle-conscious.

(109)—"o, never say . . ."

SUMMARY: *My absence from you does not mean I love you less, and though I have faults I should never dream of leaving you— my all in all.*

PARAPHRASE

1. O, never say that I was false-hearted,
2. though absence seemed to lessen my love for you:
3. I might as easily try to depart from myself
4. as from my soul, which resides in your heart.
5. In your breast is my love's home: if I have traveled about,
6. like a traveler, I always return home;
7. I return punctually, but not changed in my love by time,
8. so that I myself return to relieve the pain of absence.
9. Never believe, even if there reigned in my nature
10. all the weaknesses that beset all flesh,
11. that my nature could be so preposterously sullied
12. as to part from you for nothing, and desert all your virtuous goodness.
13.　　For I call this whole wide world nothing,
14.　　except you, my rose of beauty; in this world you are my everything.

COMMENT: Here is a familiar absence sonnet but with a difference: Shakespeare admits to a lag in his attentions to his friend and patron. There is a newer note, breathing confidence in his own powers. Perhaps he was becoming more independent economically.

(110)—"alas, 'tis true . . ."

SUMMARY: *I have been disloyal to my love, but never again, since you are my best and only love.*

PARAPHRASE

1. Alas, it is true I have traveled here and there,
2. exposing myself like a jester to the public view;
3. I have wounded my own thoughts and sold cheaply what is most dear to me;
4. I have made my old sins into new passions.
5. It is most certainly true that I have viewed your faithful love
6. as though I were a stranger; but, by heaven,
7. these trespasses have only strengthened my love;
8. and even worse sins have shown you to be my best love.
9. Now all that inconstancy is done with, and what I offer you is an eternal love:
10. My physical appetite for love never more will I put

11. to new trials in order to test the love of an older friend,
12. a god in love, to whom I am bound.
13.   Then welcome me, a welcome only second to God's in heaven,
14.   even to your most pure and loving heart.

> **COMMENT:** A revealing sonnet: Shakespeare reveals his sensitivity about the public and vulgar nature of his dramatic profession, selling cheap what is most dear. He is sensitive about exposing for the market his most intimate thoughts and making himself "a fool" before public audiences. Again there is admission of straying from the path of true love, for sexual adventures along the byways of travel. For related sonnets about his profession see 25 and 29.

(111)—"o, for my sake . . ."

SUMMARY: *My acting profession is like a brand on me, and I shall do anything to correct my failings—but your sympathy will be cure enough.*

PARAPHRASE

1. O, scold Fortune for my sake, since she is
2. the goddess who is guilty of those acts of mine which hurt you
3. in that she did not select a better profession for me than
4. acting before the public, which results in vulgar manners.
5. That is why my name is branded as vulgar,
6. and why it is that my nature is subjugated to professional acting
7. just as the dyer's hand is to dyes;
8. pity me, then, and wish me made anew—
9. while, like a willing patient, I drink up doses of
10. vinegar medicine to ward off my professional disease.
11. There is no medicine too bitter, and no
12. penance severe enough that I will not take to cure my faults.
13.   Pity me then, dear friend, and I assure you
14.   that your pity even is enough to cure me.

> **COMMENT:** See Comment on Sonnet 110. In the present sonnet we see that Shakespeare's nature is suffused like a dye with his profession. In Sonnet 29 he also refers to acting as that which he most enjoys. But if he enjoys his art, he is bitterly ashamed of its lowly social position. His social position can only be overcome ("cured") if his aristocratic friend ad-

mits him to his company and he is able to move freely among those of a more exalted social station. Here we have, perhaps, the true explanation of the whole sonnet sequence.

(112)—"your love and pity . . ."

SUMMARY: *I am deaf to all criticism or praise of me from anyone but you. To me the rest of the world is as if dead.*

PARAPHRASE

1. Your love and pity for me erase the stain,
2. which public scandal gave to my reputation;
3. for what do I care whether I am called good or bad,
4. so long as you cover up my bad and commend my good?
5. You are all the world to me, and I must strive
6. to know my faults and virtues from your mouth;
7. there is no one else I heed, no one alive,
8. who can change my hardened sense of right and wrong,
9. so profoundly do I reject the comments
10. of others, that my ears, like the unhearing adder,
11. are deaf to both critics and flatterers.
12. See how I disregard public opinion:
13.   you are so strongly ingrained in my heart
14.   that I think all the rest of the world is dead.

COMMENT: Shakespeare was evidently smarting from some attack upon his reputation (2) which was defended by his patron (4). Rowse identifies the "public scandal" as the Greene attack upon our poet in 1592 (Harper edition, p. 231).

(113)—"since I left you . . ."

SUMMARY: *I am so filled with the thought of you that the world gets distorted in my mind's eye.*

PARAPHRASE

1. Since I left you, my eyes are really in my mind,
2. and those eyes which direct my steps so I can get about,
3. have lost their ability to see, being partly blind,
4. seeming to see but effectively blinded.
5. For my eyes pass no picture to the heart

6. of bird, flower, or shape that it may lay hold of:
7. the mind can not grasp a vivid object like the eyes;
8. nor do the mind's eyes retain what they perceive.
9. For if my eyes should see the rudest or most gentle sight,
10. the loveliest or ugliest creature,
11. the mountain or the sea, the day or night,
12. the crow or the dove, the mind still shapes these things to your likeness.
13.   Thus my mind is incapable of doing anything more, and, crammed with thoughts of you,
14.   its truest part turns that which my eye sees into falsehood.

COMMENT: Here, as in the great Sonnet 97, Shakespeare shows how a mental or emotional preoccupation can distort physical perception. This idea is stated definitively by Hamlet when he says: "there is nothing either good or bad but thinking makes it so" (II,ii, 255-7).

(114)—"or whether doth my mind . . ."

SUMMARY: *Your love taught my eyes the art of alchemy, and my mind drinks up its flattery.*

PARAPHRASE

1. Is it that my mind, crowned with thoughts of you,
2. drinks up flattery, which is the plague of monarchs?
3. Or shall I say that my eyes see truly,
4. and that my love of you (like alchemy that changes base metals into gold) converts all I see into your golden image,
5. turning monsters and formless things I see
6. into sweet angels in your image,
7. converting every bad thing into perfect ones
8. as fast as objects appear before my eyes?
9. O, it is the first conjecture which is true; it is flattery in my
10. seeing, and, like a monarch requiring praise from courtiers, my mind drinks this flattery up avidly:
11. My eyes well know what is agreeable to the mind's taste,
12. and so prepares the cup of flattery to the mind's taste.
13.   If the mind is poisoned, it is a lesser sin,
14.   since my eyes love the deception and lead the mind on.

COMMENT: A very clever sonnet. The mind is first compared to a monarch who loves to be flattered (1-2), and then to a monarch, who before drinking, has his cup tasted by another to test for poisoning (10-14). Here the mind (monarch) drinks up the poison (flattery) fed to it by the eyes (the poisoner).

(115)—"those lines that I..."

SUMMARY: *Though time is a tyrant and normally alters all things for the worse, it also permits love to grow to ever greater heights.*

PARAPHRASE

1. Those lines I wrote before do lie;
2. even those lines that said I could not love you more than I do;
3. but then my mind knew no reason why
4. my full flame of love should increase after I had written those lines;
5. but time, whose casual events are reckoned in the millions,
6. makes vows invalid and changes the decrees of kings,
7. darkens the skin of the fair, dulls the most zealous,
8. and makes the strong-minded change their minds and accept time's inexorability!
9. Alas, then, why, since I fear time's inevitability,
10. could I not have said "Now I love you best,"
11. at the time when, after being uncertain of your love, I became sure of it,
12. thus glorifying my love now, uncertain of all else?
13. The answer is that love is a babe, and therefore I may not say that ("Now I love you best")
14. in order to permit full growth to a love still growing.

COMMENT: The reconciliation of the lovers after their mutual infidelities has so deepened their love that for once Shakespeare does not reject the mutability of time however powerfully he pictures it, but embraces it as a power which permits love to grow and mature.

(116)—"let me not to the marriage..."

SUMMARY: *True love is constant, loyal, unchanging and unchangeable in the face of time.*

PARAPHRASE

1. Let me not to the union of two loyal lovers of like mind

2. admit there can be obstacles to their love: love is not really
   true love
3. which changes when it is met by differing circumstances;
4. nor does it lessen under the threat of time to remove the
   beloved.
5. O, no! it is like an eternally fixed sea beacon,
6. which shines through storms but is never shaken;
7. true love is constant, like the North Star to all sea-going ships;
   a star
8. whose influence and worth is unknown to the voyagers, although its height in the sky can be reckoned.
9. True love is not subject to the decay of time, although
10. youth is subject to time's attack through age and death;
11. true love does not change with the passage of time,
12. but lasts even to the edge of destruction.
13.   If I am proved wrong in what I say,
14.   then I never wrote, nor has any man ever loved.

COMMENT: This sonnet majestically proclaims for all time
the definition of true love. Actually the kind of love celebrated
is quite unromantic. Here it stands for true friendship, man
for man, Platonic and divine. To Shakespeare, at least in the
Sonnets, such a love was not possible between man and
woman. Rowse claims that the sonnet sounds like a valedic-
tion, which is doubtful. The word *impediments* (2) seems to
have come from one of Shakespeare's favorite books, the
Book of Common Prayer: "If any of you know cause or just
impediment . . ." (from the marriage service). O. J. Campbell
calls this sonnet "the most admired and most quoted of all
the sonnets" (p. 145).

Structure: Quatrain 1 declares true love to be unchanging
and firmly founded. Quatrain 2 declares it unchangingly steady,
whose true value is unrealizable. *Quatrain* 3 says true love
is not changed by Time but is eternal, and the *Couplet* declares in an infamous letdown that it is true. The single ideal,
the definition of true love between friends, through more and
more intense imagery, reaches its superb climax in line 12.
The rest is silence—or should have been, for all that could
have been said on the subject had already been said—certainly
no jigging couplet was needed or wanted.

Imagery: Quatrain 2 compares love to a sea beacon (5) un-
shaken by tempests. Then it is compared to a star (the North
Star), which guides lost barks at sea on the right course; these

ships can measure the height of the star with a sextant but never will they learn its value or worth. Similarly true love serves as the perfect model for other lovers on earth who are guided by it, even though they may not know its true worth. The metaphor is logically superb, and superbly effective. Quatrain 3 shows that although the *rosy lips and cheeks* (9) of young lovers may be cut down by Time (who is pictured as a person mowing down wheat heads (the rosy lips and cheeks), their true love is not subject in this way to Time's bending sickle. True love may even endure beyond time to the Day of Judgment, if the phrase "edge of doom" (12) is taken in this sense.

(117)—"accuse me thus . . ."

SUMMARY: *I strayed from you, my love, only to test your constancy and loyalty to me.*

PARAPHRASE

1. Accuse me in this way: that I have been neglectful in all ways,
2. in returning the love your great worth deserves,
3. in forgetting to invoke your precious love for me,
4. to which I am tightly bound daily.
5. That I have been frequenting with strangers
6. and have voluntarily given to others the time to which you have a right;
7. that I have gone on long journeys in all directions
8. to get the farthest possible distance away from you.
9. Record carefully both my intentional and unintentional faults,
10. considering the valid circumstantial evidence against me
11. bring me within range of your frowns of disapproval,
12. but do not launch your aroused hate at me,
13.   since my appeal is that I merely strove to prove
14.   the constancy and loyalty of your love for me.

COMMENT: We suspect another break in the relationship, owing to Shakespeare's sinful conduct. There is not any doubt however, that the sonnets breathe a new confidence, lacking the note of dependence found earlier. Note the lame excuse Shakespeare gives for his conduct: that he was testing the love of his friend!

(118)—"like as to make . . ."

SUMMARY: *I take a strong physic to cure myself of a sweet and* *uncloying love; but I turn sicker, thus adding to my faults; for I learned that physics poison those already sick with love of you.*

PARAPHRASE

1. In order to increase our appetites,
2. we stimulate our jaded palates with pungent spices,
3. just as we forestall an unknown illness
4. by taking a physic, turning sick to avoid sickness.
5. Even so, after becoming fully happy in your never cloying and sweet love,
6. I directed my attention elsewhere towards bitter experiences;
7. and, sick of my fine state in your heart, I found a kind of fitness
8. in being sick, even before there was a true need for it.
9. And thus, thinking I would be prudent in my love in order to anticipate
10. illnesses not yet arrived, I fell into actual faults,
11. and brought my healthy state to one requiring a cure.
12. My love, being too full of the goodness of your love, attempted a cure through taking on an illness.
13. But from this I learned a true lesson:
14. that such physics poison him who is already sick for love of you.

COMMENT: Here Shakespeare says that by having amours elsewhere he might be able to cure himself of his great love for his friend; but the result was only a kind of poisoning. His miraculous power of turning such an ugly subject (i.e. the taking of physics) into genuine poetry is nowhere more evident. For Elizabethan purging practices see Rowse's *Ralegh and the Throckmortons*, pp. 276-7, 295. Some critics find this sonnet "disgusting."

(119)—"what potions have I drunk . . ."

SUMMARY: *My passion for another with its attendant sins has taught me to appreciate you all the more.*

PARAPHRASE

1. How many potions have I drunk of a temptress' tears
2. shed by a woman foul as hell;
3. applying fear to hope and hope to fear;

4. forever losing just when I thought I had won her over!
5. How many dreadful errors has my heart committed,
6. although my heart thought itself never so blessed!
7. How my eyes have bulged from their sockets
8. while I was beset by this mad passion for her!
9. O good result from evil: now I find it true
10. that good is made better by evil;
11. and a ruined love, when repaired anew,
12. grows more beautiful than ever and much stronger than at its inception.
13.   So I return to my true love chastened,
14.   and learn by my sins three times over what I have lost.

COMMENT: The genuinely strong spirit emerges from the experience of sinning, purged and ennobled by that experience. So Shakespeare, by plunging into sin, emerges a true lover. Although this might seem to be a bit of rationalization, the Christian would recognize that not even evil is all evil but that good may issue from it (9). Hubler has said: "The poet, like his tragic heroes, grows in wisdom and self-knowledge through error and suffering." Note that Sonnets 115-120 are unified in theme.

(120)—"that you were once unkind..."

SUMMARY: *We have both committed infidelities, but our resulting suffering recalls our own true love. Thus we are even, my sin in exchange for yours.*

PARAPHRASE

1. That you were once unkind is a help to me now,
2. and for the suffering I then did feel,
3. I must now bend under weight of the suffering for my own infidelity,
4. unless my nerves are made of brass or steel.
5. For if you were as hurt by my infidelity
6. as I by yours, you have gone through hell;
7. and I, like an unthinking tyrant, have not taken the time
8. to consider how I once suffered from your betrayal.
9. O, that our common suffering might have brought
10. me back to my senses—how hard true sorrow hits one;
11. I gave to you, and you returned to me, then,
12. the warm comfort so vital to suffering lovers.

13.   But your trespass is now a recompense:
14.   my sin excuses yours, and yours must excuse mine.

> **COMMENT:**   Shakespeare seems so confident in this sonnet
> —the tone is so bold—that one feels the old servant-master
> relationship now entirely gone. His friend's transgression might
> refer to his relations with Shakespeare's "Dark Lady" but
> there is not enough confirming evidence here.

> *Imagery:*   Sonnets 115-120 are also unified by medical ima-
> gery; *potion, purge etc.* In addition to medical imagery (12-13),
> church imagery predominates in this sonnet: *transgression*
> (3), *hell* (6), *trespass* (13).

(121)—" 'tis better to be vile..."

SUMMARY: *Those who make my sins an object of criticism
merely expose their own evil. Do not judge me, my love, by their
evil opinions—unless they see all men as evil and as always acting
so.*

PARAPHRASE

1. It is better to be immoral than to be thought so,
2. when one was not immoral and yet was reproached for being
   so;
3. and thus the proper pleasure of the immoral act is lost, which
   pleasure
4. is not that vile in our eyes, but in the interfering eyes of others.
5. For why do the false, lustful eyes of others
6. pay heed to my immoral acts?
7. Or, why are the more sinful people sent to spy on such a less
   sinful person as I,
8. people who in their sexual passions call that bad which I find
   to be good?
9. No, I am what I am; and those who aim to attack
10. my immoral acts are but exposing their own.
11. I may be honestly straight and they may be dishonestly crooked;
    and
12. therefore my acts must not be judged by their foul thoughts—
13.   unless they maintain this view—
14.   that all men are evil by nature, in which idea they exult.

> **COMMENT:**   A penetrating sonnet. Shakespeare is quite

aware of the false pretensions of mankind's "worser" sort and refuses to be judged by them: "Judge not lest ye be judged"! Also Biblical is the famous phrase in which God identifies himself to Moses: "I am that I am" (9). The tone here is bitterly sarcastic, almost caustic—a quality in which no one excels more than our poet.

(122)—"thy gift, thy tables . . ."

SUMMARY: *I gave your notebook away, which contained a record of your love; but that record is better kept in my memory—an external aid to the memory of our love would imply forgetfulness on my part.*

PARAPHRASE

1. Your gift, the notebook, is permanently kept in my brain,
2. therein inscribed immemorably:
3. its contents therein worth far more than the notebook pages themselves,
4. and will remain in my brain until eternity;
5. or, at least, so long as brain and heart
6. have the natural power to survive;
7. till each yields up to the oblivion of death itself that part
8. it contains of you, my record of you can never be missed;
9. therefore, that lesser notebook you gave me could not do so well as my memory and heart in maintaining its contents,
10. nor do I need a score sheet to sum up my love:
11. therefore, I was so bold as to give your notebook away,
12. and put my trust in my brain and heart where its recordings are much better kept.
13. To keep an outside aid to remember you
14. were to imply forgetfulness in me.

COMMENT: Just as, in Sonnet 77, we learn that Shakespeare had given a notebook with poems to his friend, so here we see that the friend had apparently also given Shakespeare a notebook for personal jottings, which Shakespeare admits here he has given away. His ingenious excuse for parting with such a precious gift is recorded in this sonnet—take it as you will.

(123)—"no, time, thou shalt not . . ."

SUMMARY: *Time's hurried course through past and present,*

bringing constant change to all life and things, makes me vow
that I shall be true to my love despite time and death itself.

PARAPHRASE

1. No, time, you shall not boast that I am subject to your changes;
2. your pyramids, built by recent strength,
3. are, to me, nothing new, nothing strange:
4. they are but fancier copies of what has been done before.
5. Our lives are brief, and so we wonder all the more at
6. whatever you foist upon us from the depths of the past;
7. and we think these new structures to be our own original
8. rather than realize that man has known of such things before.
9. I defy both Time's records and Time himself;
10. and I am amazed neither by the present nor the past;
11. for things of the past and present, Time's records are mis-
12. they come and go with your swift flight.
13.   This I do vow, which I shall always do,
14.   that I will be true to my love despite the changes of Time
      and the final death that Time brings.

COMMENT: Campbell considers the "pyramids" of line 2 to be an allusion to the obelisks erected along the street to celebrate King James royal entry (March 15, 1604), p. 152, one of a baker's dozen of similar theories. Those famous "pyramids", that have so excited the sonnet-daters, are more likely, however, to be symbolic of all those constructions man has erected in the course of time. Notice Shakespeare's essential conservatism revealed again: he does not believe in change.

(124)—"if my dear love . . ."

SUMMARY: *I am politically more astute than those whose political*
fates wax and wane: my love stands above the intrigue, affected
neither by fair nor foul politicking.

PARAPHRASE

1. If my love for you were subject to political intrigue,
2. it would (like a bastard child of Fortune) be unclaimed by you,
3. since it would be subject to the changes of the time,
4. destroyed like a weed or loved like a plucked flower.
5. But no, our friendship was not built upon the chances or changes of state;

6. it is not affected by good fortune, nor does it lessen
7. under the attacks of threatened imprisonment,
8. which seems to be the fashion nowadays.
9. It does not fear political intrigue, which like a heretic to proper government is
10. attuned only to the opportunistic moment;
11. but rather stands monumentally alone, more politically wise than ever
12. in that it is subject neither to good nor to bad political luck.
13.   In witness, I call those people dupes of time,
14.   who die martyrs of the state after living a life of crime.

COMMENT: Sonnet 123 dealt with *mutability* versus *constancy* in the course of time; in this sonnet the contrast is politically oriented. The avid sonnet-daters seize upon this sonnet as vividly autobiographical. See the Variorum edition by Hyder Rollins: "Extraordinarily numerous and divergent are the historical references that have been detected in these fourteen lines. None has been or can be proved." (I, 311-312).

(125)—"were't aught to me..."

SUMMARY: *I realize now that the honors and greatness I have achieved are unimportant, since they can be lost as easily as won, but that what is truly important is the mutual cherishing of our love.*

PARAPHRASE

1. Is it anything to me that I have paraded with the great,
2. externally honoring external pomp;
3. or that I have laid down great poems for eternity,
4. which effort has proved more vain than outright neglect?
5. Have I not seen those persons dedicated to appearances and ceremony
6. lose everything in their efforts to pay too much
7. for the sweet political plums they had expected, foregoing simple tastes,
8. pitiful show-offs, utterly empty in their hope for promotion?
9. No, let me pay my devotions to your heart:
10. and take my offerings—poor but freely given, and un-
11. adulterated, knowing no artifice, but
12. only a free mutual exchange between your self and mine.
13.   Away then with false thoughts of false ceremony! a true soul
14.   when most accused by others is least under their sway.

COMMENT: The theme is related to the preceding sonnet. As essentially the last sonnet in the series to his friend, Sonnet 125 is important: what a change from the fawning and humble deference of some of the early sonnets in this series! Here is a proudly asserted equality and a fierce independence. It is a fitting climax to the greatest series of sonnets in English. In Sonnet 126 the farewell *envoi* is given.

(126)—"o, thou, my lovely boy . . ."

SUMMARY: *Nature keeps you free of time's depredations; but she must, sooner or later, give you up to time and death—so beware of Nature!*

PARAPHRASE

1. O you, my lovely boy, who have it in your power
2. to hold back time itself—
3. you who have grown lovelier with the passing (waning) of time, and therein
4. show your lovers aging while your sweetness grows:
5. If Nature, lord over all destruction,
6. keeps preventing you from aging even as time goes on,
7. why, then, she does this to demonstrate her power
8. to hold back the dismal progress of time.
9. Yet, you must fear nature, you—her darling;
10. true, she may hold back time for you, but she can not do it forever, even for you—her very jewel!
11. Her final account to time and death must be inevitably rendered,
12. and her debt is paid up after handing you over to time and death.

COMMENT: The first thing we notice in this farewell note is that it is twelve rhymed couplets, not in the sonnet form but an *envoi*, neatly stating the primary theme of the sonnet series: time's inevitable depredations upon man and his works, and Shakespeare's efforts to preserve his friend's beauty immortally in his verse. Imagery associated with time: a *mirror* to remind the youthful of decay, a *scythe* to remind them of inevitable death through time, and an *hour-glass* to show them the deadly sliding of the minutes of their beauty; see Hubler, p. 134, who quotes the Tucker Brooke edition (1936).

(127)—"in the old age..."

SUMMARY: *My brunette is not fair, but cosmetics have made her so in the eyes of others.*

PARAPHRASE

1. In days gone by a brunette was not deemed fair,
2. or, if so, such persons were not called beautiful;
3. but now the brunette has inherited the title of beauty;
4. and natural blonde beauty itself is scorned shamefully as a product of cosmetics;
5. for since women, through the use of cosmetics, conceal their natural looks,
6. making the ugly fair-looking with paints and powders like putting on a mask,
7. lovely beauty of nature has no respect, nor worship,
8. but is disregarded, if not disgraced.
9. Hence my mistress' eyes are raven black, and
10. also her hair; both her eyes and hair seem to be in black mourning;
11. for those who were not born fair in looks can still appear to seem beautiful through cosmetics,
12. thus slandering nature's gifts with a false front.
13.   Yet the hair and eyes of my brunette mourn so prettily
14.   that everyone says she is a model of beauty.

COMMENT: Sonnets 127-154 are addressed to the poet's mistress, a dark-complexioned brunette known as the Dark Lady. In contrast to the typical Elizabethan ideal lady (blonde, fair, delicate, white, red-cheeked, rose-lipped, etc., the Petrarchan ideal being her probable original), our poet's mistress is "black" which to Shakespeare merely meant dark; but the associations the word "black" carried are multiform, as we shall see. In the first sonnet addressed to the Dark Lady Shakespeare's tone is ironic and teasing.

(128)—"how oft, when thou..."

SUMMARY: *I envy the virginal keys that receive the kisses of your fingers while you play, but I would gladly let the keys receive such kisses if I were allowed your lips.*

PARAPHRASE

1. How often, when you, my mistress, who are like music to my soul, are yourself playing music
2. upon the blissful keys of the virginal, whose mechanism resounds
3. to the touch of your sweet fingers, gently plucking
4. the virginal chords which delight my ears,
5. do I envy those keys that nimbly leap up
6. to kiss your tender palms,
7. while my poor lips, which should receive those kisses,
8. blush at the boldness of those keys.
9. My lips, to be so thrilled, would gladly change their place
10. with those dancing keys,
11. over which your fingers gently travel,
12. making the dead wooden keys more blessed than my living lips.
13. Since the naughty keys are enjoying their contact with your fingers,
14. then give them your fingers and give me your lips to kiss.

COMMENT: A clever and fetching sonnet. The tone is delightfully whimsical especially in the conceit of virginal keys pictured as thrilled by contact with female fingers. *Error:* the keys (jacks, line 5) do not pluck the strings; the quill attached to the jacks do that (but see Rollins' *Variorum*, I, on this sonnet).

(129)—"th' expense of spirit..."

SUMMARY: *The sexual act drives mankind to madness and hell—yet no man knows how to withstand its drives.*

PARAPHRASE

1. The expenditure of vital power in a shameful waste of spirit
2. is the sexual act itself; and until the consummation of sexual lust,
3. man is perjured, murderous, full of blame,
4. savage, extreme, rough, cruel, untrustworthy;
5. no sooner is his lust satisfied than it is immediately despised;
6. madly hunted for, and no sooner had and enjoyed than it is
7. madly hated—like a fish swallowing a hooked bait
8. dangled on purpose to make the swallower go mad:
9. driving men mad in its pursuit and making him mad in its possession;

10. a passionate extremity whether had, having, or in seeking sexual satisfaction;
11. a very bliss in the experience, but once tasted, a very sorrow;
12. before the act, an anticipated thrill, after consummation, a dreamlike illusion.
13. All this the world is well aware of, yet no one knows enough
14. to shun the sexual act that leads all men to hell.

COMMENT: As we will see, "hell" has a bawdy second meaning common in the Dark Lady sonnets, as in Sonnet 144,1.12. See, for example, Boccaccio's *Decameron,* Book 3, Tenth Tale, Richard Aldington translation, Garden City, 1930. The tale was a great favorite in the Renaissance, and there is no doubt that Shakespeare and his witty contemporaries enjoyed its outrageously bawdy double entendre. Certainly, the sexual meanings of pride (swelling), hell (receptacle) occur several times in the Dark Lady sonnets—as we shall see. Unlike the *Decameron* tale, Shakespeare's tone is here only partially serious, not deadly serious. Rowse (p. 268) quotes Sidney:

Thou blind man's mark, thou fool's self-chosen snare,
Fond fancy's scum, and dregs of scattered thought,
Band of all evils, cradle of causeless care,
Thou web of will, whose end is never wrought.

Yet Victorians (then and now) do not see sexual wit in this sonnet, the sparkling underneath the seriousness. Archbishop Trench, J. A. Symonds, Bernard Shaw and others find it wholly serious and immensely profound, Theodore Watts Duncan calling the sonnet "the greatest sonnet in the world"! But the tone is not too much out of key with the two previous sonnets.

Technique: This sonnet is especially effective in its use of *enjambment* or run-on lines which provides a sense of uncontrollable passion brilliantly uniting form and content.

(130)—"my mistress' eyes..."

SUMMARY: *I love my mistress, faults and all, and think her as beautiful as any man's mistress pictured falsely by exaggerated and insincere comparisons.*

PARAPHRASE

1. My mistress' eyes are not so bright as the sun's,
2. coral is far more red than her lips;

3. if snow be white, why then her breasts are dark,
4. if hairs be wires, then black wires grow on her head.
5. I have seen roses of a mingled red and white color,
6. but no such color is in her cheeks;
7. and in some perfumes there is more sweetness
8. than in the breath that my mistress exhales.
9. I love to hear her speak, yet I am well aware
10. that music is much more pleasant in sound;
11. I never saw a goddess walking, I grant, but
12. when my mistress walks she treads on the ground.
13.   And yet, by heaven, I think my love as rare
14.   as any woman described by her lover with false and insincere comparisons.

COMMENT: This sonnet is satiric, and one hopes it was circulated privately among his friends and not actually handed to his mistress. With other anti-Petrarchan poets such as Donne, Shakespeare here ridicules the Petrarchan mode of description, by now a standard cliché: the lady is a goddess, her hair golden wires (wires were used in building hair-dos), her lips red as coral, her breasts white as snow, her breath redolent of perfume, etc. Incidentally, line 4 informs us that his brunette had black hair. The remark about her breath, says Rollins (jokingly?) may refer to the mistress indulgence in the new fad of "drinking" (i.e., smoking) tobacco.

(131)—"thou art as tyrannous..."

SUMMARY: *My sighs of love disprove the slanders on your beauty—it is your deeds that give rise to the slander.*

PARAPHRASE

1. You, in your very self, are as tyrannical
2. as those women whose pride in their beauty makes them so cruel;
3. for you know very well that to my doting heart
4. you are the fairest and most precious jewel.
5. Yet, in good faith, some say that when they see you,
6. they find your beauty not enough to make lovers groan with desire:
7. I dare not be so bold as to say they are wrong,
8. although I swear it is true to myself:
9. And to corroborate that what I swear to (that you are not fair enough to make lovers sigh) is not false,

10. I heave a thousand sighs by simply thinking of your face.
11. These sighs, which I heave in quick succession, are witnesses to the truth
12. that brunettes make the fairest ladies, in my judgment.
13.   You are not dark in anything, except in your actions, and from
14.   those actions arises this slander, I believe.

COMMENT: Shakespeare is far more sincere in his mistress sonnets than in the duty-sonnets that flowered in the previous series. He is frank about her looks and her actions—and he is frank about his feelings. In these sonnets his wit constantly plays upon the paradox that "black" (dark, foul or brunette) is "fair" (light); see line 12.

(132)—"thine eyes I love..."

SUMMARY: *Your dark eyes, which seem to take pity on me, are most becoming; then let your heart do the same, and I will swear that beauty herself is ugly and all blondes similarly ugly.*

PARAPHRASE

1. I love your black eyes, which as if pitying me and
2. realizing the disdain for me in your heart,
3. have put on black for me like loving mourners,
4. looking with attractive pity upon my lover's pangs.
5. And, to tell the truth, not even the morning sun in heaven
6. adorns the grey eastern sky more beautifully than your eyes do your cheeks;
7. nor does even the brilliant evening star (Venus)
8. glorify the sombre western sky half as much as
9. your black mourning eyes become your features.
10. O, then let your heart find it as fitting
11. to mourn for me, since mourning suits you so well;
12. and let pity for me seize your entire being.
13.   Then will I swear that beauty herself is ugly,
14.   and that all those who lack your dark features are ugly too.

COMMENT: Note the punning on *morning* and *mourning* in lines 5, 9, 11. This sonnet would seem to belie all that Shakespeare swore to in his anti-Petrarchan Sonnet 130. We have the clichés all over again: the eyes adorn her cheeks like the morning sun, or like the evening star; the lady must pity her woebegone lover, etc. But there is this difference: that Shakespeare does not claim his mistress to be the ideal of beauty, and certainly not the Petrarchan ideal, but rather that she is most beautiful in his eyes, that he personally prefers her looks to that of the conventional ideal. This would seem to be a more genuinely romantic attitude.

(133)—"beshrew that heart..."

SUMMARY: *You have enslaved the hearts of my friend and me; free him and my imprisonment would not be cruel—yet it would be, for I should be all yours.*

PARAPHRASE

1. Curse that heart that makes my heart groan
2. at the deep wound it gives both my friend and me:
3. Is it not enough that you torture me with pangs of love,
4. but that my dearest friend must also be a slave to your enslavement?
5. Your cruel eyes (because they do not respond to my love) have separated me from my true self;
6. and my second self, my friend, you have even more deeply enslaved;
7. thus I am deserted by him, me, and by you—
8. a triple torment for me to be thus three times thwarted.
9. Do imprison my heart in your unfeeling breast, which is like a prison of steel;
10. but then let my heart serve as a substitute for the heart of my friend and bail his out of your imprisonment;
11. whoever imprisons me, let my heart, in turn, serve as the guardhouse of my friend;
12. you could not then make my imprisonment a harsh one;
13. and yet you will make my imprisonment cruel, since I, being imprisoned in your heart,
14. am necessarily yours, and all that I contain (my friend's heart, in particular) is also yours.

COMMENT: If the reader will refer back to Sonnets 34 and 35, he will see a similar situation described. The friend is also a paramour of the mistress—a three-pronged dilemma for poor Shakespeare.

Imagery: There is an extended conceit here in which the

lady's breast is compared to a prison which contains the hearts of Shakespeare and his friend. Shakespeare, who is more leniently imprisoned, would like to offer his own heart as bail for that of his friend and then be appointed prison guard over his friend. He thinks that this would lighten his own imprisonment, because his friend's heart would be within his own heart; but then he realizes that, since his own heart is imprisoned within his mistress's heart, this would only renew his friend's imprisonment to his mistress.

(134)—"so, now I have confessed . . ."

SUMMARY: *You have enslaved us both, even taking my friend when he had intervened for me. Now you have us both in your toils, and though he is prize enough for both of us, you keep me enchained.*

PARAPHRASE

1. So, now that I have admitted that my friend belongs to you,
2. and that I, too, am enslaved to your sexual desire;
3. I shall gladly forfeit myself to you, so that my other self, my friend,
4. is returned to me for my comfort.
5. But you will not accept me as a ransom, nor does he wish his freedom,
6. for you are greedy and he is, on the other hand, compliant;
7. he learned that in trying to help me in my affair with you
8. he too became tied to you as tightly as was I.
9. You will take advantage of your beauty
10. like a moneylender who exacts excessive usury for what he lends,
11. and then you will sue my friend who acted as security for me and thus also went into debt to you;
12. and thus I lose him through my unkind use of him.
13. I have lost my friend, you have both him and me;
14. he is enough prize for us both, but still I am not free.

COMMENT: There is important information here: Shakespeare had asked his friend to help him with the lady, who then promptly snared his would-be protector. Naturally the lady will not yield up the friend in spite of Shakespeare's plea. It is important to note that the word "will" may mean desire and, by implication, sex and appetite (2).

Imagery: mortgag'd, will, forfeit, covetous, surety-like, bond, bind, statute, use, debtor, pays, etc., are all part of an extended conceit on money lending, a favorite field for sexual word-play.

(135)—"whoever hath her wish . . ."

SUMMARY: *Why do you refuse my desires when you take on so many others—make me you sole lover to satisfy your desires.*

PARAPHRASE

1. Whoever else may have satisfied her wish, you certainly have your Will,
2. and more than your Will, and Will in overplus:
3. I, who still annoy you, am more than enough to satisfy you
4. adding my own desires to yours.
5. Will you, whose desire is large and spacious,
6. not once agree to bury my pleasure in yours?
7. Is it fair for the desires of others to seem pleasant to you,
8. but not to fairly accede to mine?
9. The sea is all water, yet it still takes in rain,
10. thus adding more water to its already abundant mass;
11. so you, being rich in Will, add to your Will
12. one desire of mine, thus making your Will larger.
13. Do not unkindly refuse fair suitors, and do
14. think they are rolled into one person, and that I am that one Will.

COMMENT: In this and the next sonnet, Shakespeare puns outrageously on his own first name, Will. In addition to the seven places in the Quarto text of this sonnet in which the name "Will" is used, there are six other times in which the uncapitalized word "will" is used. As "Will" may have also been the name of the Dark Lady's friend and, perhaps, husband, and as the word "will" is susceptible to a great many meanings, including wish, desire, sexual desire, and sexual pleasure or satisfaction, the range of punning in this sonnet is virtually unlimited. This is certainly one of the most richly ambiguous and bawdy sonnets in the sequence and suffers more than most in paraphrasing, as it loses not simply the greater beauty of Shakespeare's language but also the quality of ambiguity. To reduce this difficulty, I have retained the seven instances of the name "Will" while paraphrasing the six instances of the word "will," but it should be remembered that the name can here also suggest the other connotations of desire and pleasure and that the word also implies the name. This practice of name punning was a common one in the Renaissance. To cite but one example, Sir Philip Sidney punned on the name of his beloved's husband, "Rich," in his sonnet sequence, *Astrophel and Stella* (XXXV and XXXVII).

(136)—"if thy soul check . . ."

SUMMARY: *Admit me inconspicuously into the list of your lovers and make my name (Will) your desire.*

PARAPHRASE

1. If your conscience scolds you for my telling the truth,
2. then swear to your stubborn soul that I was your Will,
3. and the faculty of volition, as your soul well knows, is an attribute of the soul and, therefore, admitted there:
4. thus far, out of love for me, admit my request, my sweet,
5. And Will will fill your treasure-box;
6. Ay, fill it full of desires, so long as mine is one.
7. With things of great number we easily prove
8. that one is really nothing.
9. Then let me pass through uncounted with the rest,
10. though in the true record of your lovers I must be counted;
11. then think of me as nothing, so long as you do not mind
12. holding that nothing myself, which should prove a sweet some-thing to you.
13. Make but my name ["Will" also means sexual desire] your love, and love that desire always,
14. and then you will have to love me, for my name is Will.

COMMENT: See Comment to Sonnet 135 for the punning possibilities on "Will" and "will."

(137)—"thou blind fool, love . . ."

SUMMARY: *Why has Cupid blinded me so that I see things distortedly; such as my mistress—who is not only my private park but is also a public thoroughfare.*

PARAPHRASE

1. You blind fool, Cupid, what are you doing to my eyes

2. that they behold things and yet see them not as they are?
3. My eyes know what beauty is like; they see its place;
4. yet they take the worst in beauty to be the best.
5. If my eyes, distorted by overpartial love,
6. be fastened on the sex of my love (which is like a bay in which all men go sailing)
7. why have you made of the false vision of my eyes hooks
8. to tie up my heart's judgment?
9. Why should my heart think that my mistress
10. is only for my use, when she is used as much as a public park?
11. Or is it that my eyes seeing this, say it is not so,
12. in order to imply fair truth to such a foul face?
13.   In truthful matters my eyes and heart have erred,
14.   and both are now devoted to this false plague, my mistress.

COMMENT: There is no doubt about it, the Dark Lady is grossly promiscuous. After the two highly comic and bawdy *will* sonnets (135-136), we have Shakespeare vituperatively serious. His blind passion makes him see his whore as a lady.

Good but bawdy: "the bay where all men ride." Incidentally that *false plague* (14) could also refer to venereal disease, which she may have had.

(138)—"when my love swears..."

SUMMARY: *My love and I both lie glibly to each other, she by concealing her whoredom and I about my age—but our common lies grease the paths of our love.*

PARAPHRASE

1. When my love swears that she is truthful,
2. I believe her, though I know she lies,
3. so that she might think me some inexperienced youth,
4. unaware of the world's false subtleties.
5. Thus I act as if I thought she thinks me to be young,
6. even though she knows I have passed my prime;
7. I go on pretending simplemindedly to believe her lies, and
8. on both sides simple truth-telling is concealed.
9. But why does she not state that she is disloyal in love?
10. And why do I not tell her that I am old?
11. O, yes, love's best virtue is in the pretense of faithfulness,
12. and where love is concerned, one's age is best left uncounted.

13. Therefore I lie to her (and with her) and she with me,
14. and we conceal our respective faults with lies and go on flattering each other.

COMMENT: This is a rather touching sonnet. The Dark Lady is now Shakespeare's mistress and he her devoted slave. Both lie pitifully, but since the word "lie", a mistruth, also means sexual intercourse, there is also some comic punning here, particularly in line 13. Another version of this sonnet was printed in *The Passionate Pilgrim*, 1599.

Great line: "O, love's best habit is in seeming trust" in which the wisdom of the world is concealed.

(139)—"o, call not me..."

SUMMARY: *My mistress flirts with others, yet she does not tell me, although her eyes continue to rove elsewhere to undo other men. Best kill me with looks now and end my jealous suffering.*

PARAPHRASE

1. O, do not call on me to justify the wrong
2. that your infidelity does to my heart;
3. wound me not with flirting eyes, but with a tongue lashing.
4. Use your love's power directly—do not hurt me with tricks.
5. Then tell me you love others, but while with me,
6. dear heart, refrain from looking elsewhere to flirt.
7. Why must you hurt me with tricks, when your love's force
8. is stronger than my defenses can withstand?
9. Let me excuse you; ah, my mistress knows well enough
10. that her pretty face has been my enemy (in that I was lured to her side through them)
11. and therefore she turns her eyes away from me,
12. so that they might dart elsewhere and lure other men:
13. Yet do not look elsewhere, but since I am nearly dead with desire,
14. kill me outright by looking only at me and end my pain.

COMMENT: Shakespeare reveals great suffering from this flirtatious slut, but this does not prevent him from handling the subject of his jealousy with wit. Since his mistress's eyes attract him so fatally, he excuses her flirtatiousness by saying that it protects him from their direct power. But when he invokes her to destroy him outright by looking only at him, the ending of his pain would not only signify his destruction (by enslavement to his passion) but also his pleasure.

(140)—"be wise as thou art cruel . . ."

SUMMARY: *Be wise and tell me you love me even though you do not. Without assurance from you I may go mad with despair and slander you.*

PARAPHRASE

1. Be as wise as you are cruel; do not tax
2. my silent patience with too much disdain,
3. lest sorrow lend me words and my words express
4. how my pain arose from your lack of pity.
5. If I might teach you wisdom—it were better, my love,
6. to tell me you love me, even though you do not,
7. just as peevish sick men, nearing death,
8. hear only about their recovery from their physicians.
9. For if I should despair of your love, I should go mad,
10. and in my madness I might speak evilly about you;
11. now that this world, which sees all in a bad light, has become so evil
12. evil slander is believed by evil people.
13. So that I may not turn into such a slanderer, nor you be so slandered,
14. you must look straight ahead with your eyes, even though your love strays elsewhere.

COMMENT: Line 12 might read: mad slanderers are believed by the ears of those not astute enough to recognize that I am slandering you (Hubler, p. 150). Since the Dark Lady apparently has a reputation to preserve, she is obviously not a common, lower class whore, however promiscuous her behavior.

(141)—"in faith, I do . . ."

SUMMARY: *My five wits and senses find you abhorrent, but I am nevertheless your love-slave even though you unman me.*

PARAPHRASE

1. In faith, I do not love you from what I see,

2. for I note in your appearance many faults;
3. but it is my heart that loves what my eyes find despicable;
4. and my heart prefers to dote on you in spite of what I see.
5. Nor are my ears pleased with the sound of your voice;
6. nor is my delicate sense of feeling prone to your vulgar touches;
7. nor do my senses of taste or smell wish to be subject
8. to any feast of tasting and smelling with you.
9. Yet, neither my five wits nor my five senses can
10. dissuade my foolish heart from serving you,
11. while leaving me only the outer likeness of a man, one not in command of himself:
12. the slave-in-love of your proud heart, and your wretched vassal.
13.   Thus far my only gain is my plaguey misery,
14.   that she who makes me sin gives me pain as a reward.

COMMENT: "Plague" = disease = venereal disease (13). O. J. Campbell interprets the couplet as follows: "in a flash of spiritual insight he confesses that his sinning has been a boon to him because it serves as purgatorial punishment" (Bantam edition, p. 170). But this couplet may also be taken ironically.

(142)—"love is my sin . . ."

SUMMARY: *My sin is love for you, but even as I gaze, you flirt with others. Have pity in your heart so that you, too, may deserve pity in return.*

PARAPHRASE

1. Love is my sin, and your only virtue is hate:
2. your hatred of my passion for you, grounded on adulterous love.
3. But with my state compare your own condition,
4. and you will find it does not deserve blame;
5. or if it does, not at least from your own lips
6. that have disgraced their attractive redness,
7. kissed (like a seal on a document) other lips as often as I have; and
8. stolen men from their domestic beds.
9. Let me then in truth love you as much as you love those
10. whom your eyes woo, while mine beg a response from you;
11. put pity in your heart so that when it grows warmer in love,
12. you will then deserve to be pitied.
13.   If you seek the love you withhold from me
14.   You may be refused as befitting your own example.

COMMENT: The virtue of the Dark Lady sonnets is their stark realism and their clear-eyed vision of life.

Imagery: bonds, revenues, rents imply the counting house again: she has perhaps stolen other husbands from the beds of their wives to whom the husbands should have rightfully "paid their rents." Shakespeare, of course, was also married, though his wife, who was eight years older than he, lived apart from him in Stratford with their children during this period.

(143)—"lo, as a careful housewife..."

SUMMARY: *Please play the mother's role and return to console me, your wailing neglected lover.*

PARAPHRASE

1. Just as a thrifty housewife, running to catch
2. one of her chickens scampering away,
3. sets her babe down and hastens
4. after the chicken she wants back, during
5. which time her disregarded babe chases behind,
6. crying after her, while her chief aim is
7. to follow that which flies before her,
8. not considering her poor babe's wailing important:
9. In the same way do you chase after that which flees from you,
10. while I, like the babe, chase after you far behind.
11. Should you catch your prize, turn back to me
12. and like a mother kiss me and be kind.
13. So I will pray that you may have your way (Will);
14. if you turn back to me and still my loud wailing for you.

COMMENT: The homely image of a thrifty housewife is earthy farmyard realism, simple and direct, vivid and highly comic. Shakespeare can see himself wryly in this light. The chicken his mistress is chasing is, of course, his friend. In line 13, Shakespeare again puns on his name, with the meaning that if she has her "Will", they will both be satisfied.

(144)—"two loves I have..."

SUMMARY: *Two opposing spirits live within me, the good hand-*

some spirit I suspect of having been lured to sexual evil by the dark, evil female spirit.

PARAPHRASE

1. I have two loves, one of comfort and one of despair,
2. which like two spirits (one angelic and the other devilish) always prompt my soul;
3. the better spirit is a handsome youth;
4. the more evil spirit is a dark woman.
5. My female evil spirit, in order to win me soon to hell,
6. keeps tempting my better angelic spirit away from my side,
7. intending to corrupt my saintly spirit to turn to sinful acts,
8. luring his pure nature to her foul lust.
9. And whether my angel spirit be turned into a fiend,
10. though I suspect it, yet I cannot exactly tell whether it is true;
11. but since both are together, far from me, intimately close,
12. I guess that my good angel is deep within my evil spirit's hell.
13.   Yet I shall never be sure, always in doubt,
14.   until my bad angel purge out (or perhaps venereally infect) my good one.

COMMENT: Sonnet 143 is a kind of harbinger in theme of this sonnet but their tones are different. Here it is serious except for the brilliant turn to wit by the pun in the twelfth line. See commentary on Sonnet 129 for a fuller discussion of the origin of the use of the word *hell* to mean female vulva. Read also Sonnets 40-42 for versions of the same theme. Line 14 *fire out* directly implies venereal infection, the curse of Elizabethan London. This sonnet is a key one since it summarizes the entire sequence. One version is found in *The Passionate Pilgrim,* 1599. See Introduction.

(145)—"those lips that love's..."

SUMMARY: *My love took mercy on me by adding "not you" to her constant replies of "I hate."*

PARAPHRASE

1. Those lips of my love, made by the goddess Venus' own hand,
2. uttered "I hate"
3. to me, who pined for her love;
4. but when she saw my woeful state,

5. she immediately had mercy upon me,
6. softening her sweet words of "I hate,"
7. that were used to pronounce gentle censure upon her lovers,
8. and teaching her lips to say something new
9. by adding words to "I hate"
10. that followed, as a gentle day
11. follows night, which like a devil
12. flew away from heaven to hell:
13.   "I hate" she separated from hate, thus
14.   saving my life by adding "not you."

COMMENT: This sonnet is unique in its rhythm: it has only four iambic feet called *iambic tetrameter:* ∪ ⁄ | ∪ ⁄ | ∪ ⁄ | ∪ ⁄. It seems different in theme, as if inserted against the grain. I think it follows Sonnet 144 quite easily, even though the tone here is whimsical; note the use of *hell* in much the double sense found in line 12 of Sonnet 144. This is true also of the use of the word *fiend* (11). In addition the Dark Lady here grants the poet the pity he had formerly pleaded for in Sonnets 140 and 142.

(146)—"poor soul, the center . . ."

SUMMARY: *My soul, spend your efforts not on bodily comforts, which lead all men to death, but on your spiritual comfort—which leads to eternal life.*

PARAPHRASE

1. Poor soul, the center of my sinful body,
2. cheated by the rebellious flesh that encloses you;
3. why do you pine within and suffer poverty,
4. while spending so much on costly clothing to adorn your body?
5. Why such a great expense, when life is so short,
6. do you waste upon the swiftly aging body?
7. Shall grave worms, the inheritors of the body's corpse,
8. be eating up all your efforts? Is this the body's destiny?
9. Then, my soul, live at the expense of the body's losses,
10. and let the body waste away in order to increase your supply of virtue;
11. achieve divine rewards by dispensing with temporal waste;
12. be contented within yourself, my soul, and pay no heed to bodily show and ease.
13.   Thus you will nourish your soul upon the thought of death, which devours the bodies of men,

14.   and, having defeated spiritual death, you will achieve im-
       mortal life.

COMMENT: This is a most important sonnet of the sequence
because, in it, Shakespeare makes his most serious and direct
profession of religious faith, with particular regard to the
reality of heavenly rewards for the righteous. This belief would
seem to go against the general drift of the sonnets with their
emphasis on mutability and the finality of death, a human condition which defeats youth and beauty but which also permits
love to grow and confers upon it a tragic value. As Shakespeare
says in Sonnet 73, it is the perception of ultimate loss which
gives love its true preciousness: "This thou perceiv'st, which
makes thy love more strong,/To love that well which thou
must leave ere long." This apparent contradiction reflects the
spiritual tension of the age in which Shakespeare lived, for
Shakespeare was caught in the Renaissance tension between
the new enlightenment and the old religious faith. Though
the sonnets have been primarily directed towards the sphere
of earthly existence, with all its anxieties and joys, he here
turns from his worldly orientation in a traditional *contemptus
mundi,* (contempt for the world) holding man's primary re-
sponsibility to be the otherworldly destiny of his soul, a destiny
which can only be blessed if he rejects the pleasures of this
world. But this is not an isolated sonnet. Even in such a
mutability sonnet as 55, which claims that only the immortalizing power of his poetry can preserve his friend from
the oblivion of death, Shakespeare concludes: "So, till the
judgment that yourself arise,/You live in this, and dwell in
lovers' eyes." Here the apparent conflict would seem to be
resolved: death is only a reality until the last judgment at the
end of the world.

(147)—"my love is as..."

SUMMARY: *My sexual desire has rejected my reason's advice,
thus enraging my sexual appetite for you, the essence of evil itself.*

PARAPHRASE

1. My love for my mistress is like a fever, ever hungering
2. for that which prolongs the infection,
3. that pleasure which preserves my illness
4. in order to satisfy my uncertain and diseased appetite.

5. My reason, like a lover's physician,
6. angry that his prescriptions are not taken,
7. has abandoned me; and now I am desperately trying
8. to prove by my actions that sexual desire, which had rejected reason's medicine, leads to death.
9. Now I am past curing, and my reason is past caring;
10. and I am madly frantic with a continuous and feverish unrest;
11. My thoughts and speech are like a madman's,
12. at variance with truth, and mouthed like a fool's.
13.   For I have sworn you are fair and shining in goodness,
14.   but you are as evil as hell and dark as night.

COMMENT: The madly feverish poet has here written a sternly logical sonnet couched in a brilliant conceit: his sexual passion is compared to a fever, the source of which is the spiritual and perhaps also physical disease spread by his mistress; and the faculty of reason is the physician prescribing medicine to cure the fever, which the patient fiercely rejects. This sonnet is as religious in its spiritual concern as the previous sonnet, but here the poet approaches the religious belief that the wages of sin is death for he finds himself unable to reject or even control the maddening passion which has set him at variance with his better self and religious Heals. His present torment has taught him the truth of his devout belief that sin is its own punishment, but this perception has no power to influence his behavior.

Key to the imagery: fever, disease, ill, sickly, reason, prescriptions, physic, cure, care; here, the conceit is perfectly suited to the context.

(148)—"o me, what eyes . . ."

SUMMARY: *My eyes see things incorrectly as a result of my passion's clouding of their vision, and hence I perceive not the open faults of my mistress.*

PARAPHRASE

1. O me! what sort of eyes has love put into my head;
2. eyes which do not see correctly what is before them;
3. or, if they do see correctly, where has my good judgment fled,
4. which falsely condemns what my eyes do correctly see?
5. If she is lovely, upon whom my false-seeing eyes dote,

6. why do men say she is not?
7. If she is not lovely, then my love indicates quite well
8. that the approving eyes of the lover are not so accurate as that of all other men who view her negatively.
9. How can it be so? O, how can the lover's eyes see correctly,
10. when he is so affected in gazing at and weeping for his mistress?
11. No wonder, then, that I see incorrectly when I look at her;
12. even the sun can not see clearly until the clouds go away.
13.   O cunning love, I am kept blinded by my own tears of desire and frustration,
14.   lest I should with correct-seeing eyes discover your sinful faults.

COMMENT: A favorite theme reappears here, one that dominates his plays as well: the discrepancy between the reality and the appearance, between exterior show and inner truth, here shown again to be the distorting effect of the emotions upon perception. See also Sonnets 127, 131, 132, and 141.

(149)—"canst thou, o cruel . . ."

SUMMARY: *I love you completely and take your side even against myself; but you go on hating me; now I know I am blind, since those who can see correctly what you really are like, are the ones you love.*

PARAPHRASE

1. Can you, my cruel mistress, say I do not love you,
2. when I against my self take sides with you?
3. Do I not think of you when I forget
4. myself completely for your sake?
5. Do I call anyone who hates you my friend?
6. Do I fawn upon anyone of whom you disapprove?
7. No! if you frown upon me, do I not take
8. revenge upon myself through my suffering?
9. There is no quality in my respected self
10. which is too proud to serve you,
11. when all the best in me worships even your faults,
12. my best being under the domination of your eyes?
13.   But my love, go on hating me, for now I know your mind;
14.   those who see correctly what you are, are the very ones you love—but I am blind.

COMMENT: This sonnet follows close upon 148 in theme. Again we see a man (our poet) madly infatuated, yet able at the same time to see the inner truth of things. It is blindness with self knowledge. Except for the astronomy metaphor in line 12 "the *motion* of thine *eyes,*" which were thought of as revolving in their "spheres", this sonnet is bare and clear, terse and emotional. But many of Shakespeare's best sonnets are naked of metaphor.

(150)—"o, from what pow'r..."

SUMMARY: *Where do you get the power to sway my heart, which looks upon your evil as good? If I love that which others abhor, I am then more worthy of your love.*

PARAPHRASE

1. Oh, from what source do you get the power
2. to dominate my heart with such an insufficient object?
3. Where do you get the power to make me see falsely,
4. and swear that light is not part of the day?
5. From where do you get your ability to make sinful things seem good,
6. so that in the worst of your acts
7. you show such sureness and skill,
8. that in my mind your worst betters the best of others?
9. Who taught you how to make me love you more,
10. in spite of the fact that I see always more reason to hate you.
11. Yet, though I love what other people hate,
12. you should not along with others, abhor my condition;
13. if your lack of worth gave rise to love in me,
14. I am the more worthy to be loved by you.

COMMENT: It is obvious that the source of his mistress' power over Shakespeare is the terrible and destructive appeal of sexual appetite. Shakespeare has clarified not only for his patron-rival-betrayer but for all mankind the inexorability of that drive so opposed to reason and intelligence.

(151)—"love is too young..."

SUMMARY: *Awareness is born of love, and my sexual flesh, awakened by my soul, conquers and serves your sex in a proud rise and dejected fall at your side.*

PARAPHRASE

1. Love is too young to know what awareness is;
2. yet who does not know that awareness is born of love?
3. Then, gentle cheater, do not press charges against me,
4. lest your sweet self prove guilty of the charges;
5. for, since you betray me, I betray
6. my soul to my body's sexual treason:
7. my soul tells my flesh that it is allowed to make
8. a sexual conquest—and my organ waits no longer,
9. but rising up at the sound of your name points at you
10. as his battle prize. Swollen with pride,
11. it is then glad to serve as your poor drudge,
12. taking an erect stand in your sexual affairs and then falling limp at your side.
13. Do not hold that I lack feeling when I call
14. my mistress "love," for whose dear love my flesh proudly rises and falls.

COMMENT: The most bawdy sonnet of the entire 154! The elemental description contained within this sonnet is absolutely delightful in its whimsy and wit.

Imagery: The soul is pictured as a military commander inciting the body to triumph on the battlefield of sexual *intercourse* with the mistress, to stand therein and eventually fall by her side. Bawdy, witty, but not leering.

(152)—"in loving thee thou know'st..."

SUMMARY: *I have sworn oaths to your love and faith, truth and constancy, which were lies to eyes that could see, unlike mine; and my oath that you are good and fair makes me even a greater liar.*

PARAPHRASE

1. You know that in loving I have betrayed my wife;
2. but you are a double betrayer in swearing that you love me;
3. by your act, first breaking your own marriage vow and then breaking your oath of faith to me,
4. vowing new hate for me after a recent reconciliation.
5. But why do I accuse you of breaking two vows
6. when I break twenty? I am the one who is most perjured,
7. since all my vows are oaths, made merely to deceive you;

8. and all my honest faith in you is lost;
9. for I have sworn solemn oaths as to your deep affection,
10. love, truth, and constancy;
11. and to shed light upon you, I did not let my eyes see truly, as though blind,
12. or made them falsely deny the truth of the things they saw.
13.   For I have sworn you to be good and fair: then the greater perjurer I (or my eye)
14.   to swear so foul a lying oath.

COMMENT: After a reconciliation, his mistress is again disloyal to Shakespeare. Appropriately, one feels that in this, essentially the last sonnet in the Dark Lady series, Shakespeare is about to walk off in disgust—certainly not a very grand climax to the greatest sonnet sequence in English!

(153)—"cupid laid by . . ."

SUMMARY: *Cupid's torch believed quenched is fired anew by your eyes.*

PARAPHRASE

1. Cupid laid aside his torch of love and fell asleep:
2. one of Diana's maids, finding a chance to steal his torch,
3. quickly steeped it,
4. in a cold fountain of the valley,
5. which took on from the torch a fire of holy love,
6. eternal and full of life;
7. the fountain became a hot boiling bath, which men to this day try
8. as an effective cure for strange diseases.
9. But upon seeing my mistress, Cupid's torch became aflame again,
10. the boy Cupid having as an experiment touched my breast with passion:
11. I, feverish with desire, desired the help of the curative bath
12. and went there—a feverishly sad guest.
13.   But I found no cure; the bath which alone can aid me lies
14.   in the place where Cupid himself was fired anew with passion
        —in the eyes of my mistress.

COMMENT: Sonnets 153 and 154 are conventional in theme, forming a kind of epilogue to the Dark Lady series (127-154).

Both these sonnets are free translations of a fifth century epigram by the Grecian, Marianus Scholisticus. Bath was a curative resort for ills, and perhaps these two sonnets were written for some lady visiting the place. But an alternative interpretation is that Shakespeare himself tried the curative powers of that resort to restore himself from passionate involvement with the Dark Lady. Still others say that the theme of these sonnets is so remote from the series that they are probably not Shakespeare's.

(154)—"the little love-god..."

SUMMARY: *Same as 153, which see.*

PARAPHRASE

1. The little love-god Cupid lying once upon a time asleep,
2. laid by his side his heart-inflaming torch,
3. while many virgin nymphs of Diana's train who had vowed to remain chaste,
4. come passing by; but in her virgin hand
5. the most beautiful nymph took up the torch of fire
6. which many legions of loyal hearts had fired up;
7. and so the chief instiller of hot sexual desire (Cupid)
8. was while sleeping disarmed by a virgin.
9. This torch she quenched in a cool well nearby,
10. which well took fire from the perpetual heat of the torch,
11. turning into a medical bath
12. for the use of men diseased; but I, my mistress' slave,
13. went to Bath for a cure, and I found the following:
14. Love's torch of fire heats water, but water does not succeed in cooling passion.

COMMENT: The fact that this sonnet was so popular in Elizabethan times is natural; it is straightforward bawdry.

THE SONNETS AND THE CRITICS: *A SURVEY**

SIXTEENTH CENTURY: *Francis Meres:* In 1598 Francis Meres wrote his *Palladis Tamia: Wits Treasury,* wherein he comments upon Shakespeare's passing his "sugared sonnets among his private friends." This indicates that Shakespeare circulated his sonnets among his private friends in manuscript, his aim being to win their esteem and praise. Poetic activity was, unlike playwriting, a gentleman's occupation in which there was to be no monetary reward for labor spent upon the Muse. To print the poems for sale would have been vulgar; this is why they were passed among his friends in handwritten originals or copies of the originals. Certainly, a man's reputation as a writer could be quite materially enhanced by the circulation of manuscript poems.

SEVENTEENTH CENTURY: *John Benson:* In 1640 Benson published a small volume of poetry entitled *Poems: Written by Wil. Shake-speare. Gent.* It was a piratical venture since Benson did not own the copyright to the poems. What is interesting in this volume is the preface addressed to the reader. Benson calls Shakespeare's sonnets "seren, cleere and eligantly plaine, such gentle straines as shall recreate and not perplexe your braine, no intricate or cloudy stuffe to puzzell intellect, but perfect eloquence . . ." A small number of the sonnets are indeed "seren, clear and elegantly plain," but by far the larger number are among Shakespeare's most intricate writing; the clarification of the sonnet's linguistic intricacies was the primary aim for the publication of this book.

EIGHTEENTH CENTURY: In his preface to *The Plays of William Shakespeare* (1793) *Steevens* has nothing but contempt for the sonnets of Shakespeare:

> We have not reprinted the Sonnets, &c. of Shakespeare because the strongest act of Parliament that could be framed, would fail to compel readers into their service . . . Had Shakespeare produced no other works than these, his name would have reached us with as little celebrity as time has conferred on that of Thomas Watson, an older and much more elegant sonnetteer.

NINETEENTH CENTURY: The nineteenth century is lavish in its praise of the sonnets of Shakespeare; and for the first time they are genuinely appreciated in praise which is often uncritically fulsome. *Samuel Taylor Coleridge* entered in the marginalia on his copy of R. Anderson's *British Poets* (1803) his support for the theory that Shakespeare's love for the young man was platonic only:

> It is noticeable that not even an allusion to that very worst of all

---

* See introduction for critical material not discussed in this section.

possible vices (for it is wise to think of the disposition, as a *vice*, not of the absurd and despicable act, as a *crime*) not even any allusion to it occurs in all his numerous plays—whereas Jonson, Beaumont and Fletcher, and Massinger are full of them . . . how impossible it was for a Shakespeare not to have been in his heart's heart chaste. I see no elaborate obscurity and very little quaintness—nor do I know any sonnets that will bear such frequent reperusal: so rich in meter, so full of thought and *exquisitest* diction . . . These sonnets, like the Venus and Adonis, and the Rape of Lucrece, are characterized by boundless fertility and labored condensation of thought, with perfection of sweetness in rhythm and meter.

John Keats: In a letter to John Reynolds, November 22, 1817, says that

. . . One of the three Books I have with me is Shakespeare's Poems: I never found so many beauties in the sonnets—they seem to be full of fine things said unintentionally . . . He has left nothing to say about nothing or anything . . .

Henry Hallam: In his *Introduction to the Literature of Europe in the Fifteenth, Sixteenth, and Seventeenth Centuries* (III, 1863 253 ff.) suspects Shakespeare's love for the young man to be too ardent, more love than was comfortable within the conventions of the time:

Notwithstanding the frequent beauties of these sonnets, the pleasure of their perusal is greatly diminished by these circumstances; and it is impossible not to wish that Shakespeare had never written them . . . But there are also faults of a merely critical nature. The obscurity is often such as only conjecture can penetrate . . . and so many frigid conceits are scattered around, that we might almost fancy the poet to have written without genuine emotion, did not such a host of other passages attest the contrary.

TWENTIETH CENTURY: *Leslie Hotson* in his *Shakespeare's Sonnets Dated: And Other Essays* (1949) claimed to have discovered the immediate historical allusions to contemporary events mentioned in such sonnets as 107, 123, and 124:

Here is a fact of cardinal importance. It indicates that *Shakespeare completed this main group of his sonnets by 1589.* The evidence has led us to a revolutionary conclusion. Heretofore, theory has put the completion of the Sonnets anywhere from 1596 to 1603—from Shakespeare's thirty-third to his fortieth year . . . The grand point which now rises to dwarf all else is the new knowledge . . . that *Shakespeare's power had reached maturity by the time he was no more than twenty-five years old.*

F. W. Bateson in an essay entitled "Elementary, My Dear Hotson!

A Caveat for Literary Detectives" (*Essays in Criticism*, I (1951), 81 ff., offers a brilliant reply to Hotson:

> Or, to put it more precisely, does the meaning now assigned to the particular phrase or passage reinforce or contradict the poetic argument of the work as a whole? It must be said that by this test the Hotson interpretation, ingenious though it is, hasn't a leg to stand on. . . . No, literary detection is a harmless avocation . . . But the game has certain elementary rules. One of them is that in the assessment of clues the primacy must always be accorded to the literary fact.

Edward Hubler in his *The Sense of Shakespeare's Sonnets*, pp. 38-63 (1952), finds that

> There is nothing like the woman of Shakespeare's sonnets in all the sonnet literature of the Renaissance . . . In all truth there is very little in the Dark Lady Sonnets which fails . . . Shakespeare's passion for the Dark Lady found its only joyous expression in comedy and word-play . . . The point is that the poet's relationship with the Dark Lady is neither dignified nor prettified; there is not a glimmer of romance.

Patrick Cruttwell discusses "Shakespeare's Sonnets and the 1590's" in a penetrating essay on the old and the new in Shakespeare's sonnets of the 1590's. See his *The Shakespearean Moment: and its Place in the Poetry of the 17th Century*, pp. 1-16., 155.

G. Wilson Knight's essay, "Time and Eternity" [Part I, Chapter IV, of *The Mutual Flame* (1955)], is a brilliant analysis of the pattern of imagery and symbol in the Sonnets.

J. W. Lever's essay "The Poet in Absence" (from *The Elizabethan Love Sonnet* (1956), is one of the very best discussions available on the "absence" sonnets, their structure, meaning, the pattern of their conceits etc. In particular, he discusses Numbers 24, 46, 47, 50, 51, 44, 45, 27, 28, 43, 61 in that order:

> There is a clear unity of development from the first heart-and-eyes conceit of XXIV, with its superfluous cleverness, to the psychological penetration of this, [i.e., no. 61] last sonnet.

John Crowe Ransom in his *The World's Body* (1937) discussed the sonnets in a chapter entitled "Shakespeare at Sonnets." Mr. Ransom, a so-called "New Critic," found the sonnets deficient in many ways:

> . . . generally they are ill-constructed . . . About a third of the sonnets of Shakespeare are fairly unexceptionable in having just such a logical structure. About half of them might be said to be tolerably workmanlike in this respect; and about half of them are seriously defective.

He went on to say that in only a minority of the sonnets is there "perfect adaptation of the logic to the meter . . . "Structurally, Shakespeare is a careless workman." His poetry is imprecise and the "only precision it has is metrical, therefore adventitious." Ransom continues:

> Those perfect sonnets are not many. It is not a wild generalization, when we look at the sonnets, to say that Shakespeare was not habitually a perfectionist; he was not a Ben Jonson, or Marvell, or Milton, and he was not a Pope.

To Ransom, John Donne was the superior poet, the more original, the firmer architect in the lyric; and above all, Donne was by far Shakespeare's better as a writer of metaphysical poetry.

Robert Graves and *Laura Riding* in their *Survey of Modernist Poetry* (1927) wrote an essay entitled "A Study in Original Punctuation and Spelling: Sonnet 129" in which they attacked the Shakespearean editors for their changes of Shakespeare's spelling and pronunciation, and for their "hundreds of unjustifiable emendations and "modernizations."

> Mr. Cummings [i.e., E. E. Cummings, the poet] and Shakespeare have in common a deadly accuracy. It frightens Mr. Cummings' public and provoked Shakespeare's eighteenth-century editors to meddle with his texts as being too difficult to print as they were written.

Like Cummings, Shakespeare expressed himself accurately and precisely in the common form of his time. The authors analyzed Sonnet 129, first in a "modernized" version, and secondly in the original version as Shakespeare wrote it [i.e., the 1609 edition of the Sonnets]:

> The failure of imagination and knowledge in Shakespeare's editors has reduced his sonnets to the indignity of being easy for everybody.

Modern editors have changed spellings, pronunciations, punctuations, arrangement of lines, etc. so that the delicate meanings, rhythms and stresses have been obscured or eliminated. Obviously the authors would prefer the 1609 edition with only the most necessary of changes from text to be allowed. The essay has had a profound influence on the editing of the Sonnets [see, for example, *A Casebook on Shakespeare's Sonnets,* edited by G. Willen and Victor B. Reed, (1964)].

Other outstanding essays on the sonnets of Shakespeare are those by Yvor Winters[1], William Empson[2], Arthur Mizener[3], Winifred M. T. Nowottny[4], and C. L. Barber[5].

[1]"Poetic Style in Shakespeare's Sonnets" from *Four Poets on Poetry,* ed. D. C. Allen (1959).

[2]"Some Types of Ambiguity in Shakespeare's Sonnets" from *Seven Types of Ambiguity* (1930).

[3]"The Structure of Figurative Language in Shakespeare's Sonnets" from *The Southern Review*, V, (1940), 730-747.

[4]"Formal Elements in Shakespeare's Sonnets" from *Essays in Criticism*, II, (1952), 76-84.

[5]"The Sonnet as an Action" from *The Sonnets of Shakespeare* (1960).

QUESTIONS AND ANSWERS ON THE
SONNETS: A REVIEW

Discuss the Renaissance attitude towards the composition of poetry.

In the Renaissance it was expected that every cultivated gentleman should be able to compose a poem or two. Indeed, it became the custom in the Renaissance for true gentlemen to write letters to their friends in verse form. Manuscripts of these "verse-epistles" circulated quite freely among friends and acquaintances. Moreover, if someone were particularly proud of his verses, he would allow *his* friends to copy the poems frim manuscript and circulate them further. In this way, a reputation as a poet might be achieved by merely the passing around of the manuscript and copies of one's verses. Shakespeare, altdough not a member of the true aristocracy himself, achieved a reputation in tris manner, aside and above his professional reputation as a writer of "common" plays for the "vulgar" public.

Discuss the publication of Shakespeare's Sonnets.

We know that Shakespeare's "sugared sonnets" were circulating in manuscript as early as 1598 because a contemporary of Shakespeare's (Francis Meres) published a kind of history of literary criticism under the title of *Palladis Tamia* (*Wit's Treasury,* 1598) in which he alludes to Shakespeare's sonnets.

Nevertheless, the Sonnets were not actually *published* until eleven years later (1609) by a not very reputable publisher called Thomas Thorpe, who printed them without Shakespeare's authorization. That is why the Thorpe edition contains many errors since the author of the Sonnets had no hand in their publication. Thorpe, then, arranged the Sonnets in what seemed to him to be a logical order and had them printed by George Eld.

Discuss the thorny problem of the "order" of the Sonnets.

1. Some of the Sonnets seem to fall in small groups indicating some kind of order, but overall there is certainly no kind of ordered plot or "sequence" to the Sonnets telling some kind of developed tale (only by inference is there a rough kind of story).
2. The sonnets do fall into three distinct and coherent groups:

   a. 1-126.
   b. 127-152.
   c. 153-154.

The first two groups are addressed to a young friend of Shakespeare's, and to his mistress—in that order. The third group is made up simply of

151

two sonnets freely translating two poems by an ancient Greek writer named Marianus, and were included by Thorpe in spite of their utter dissimilarity to the rest of the Sonnets, possibly because nothing was to be omitted that had been composed by Shakespeare even if they were simply on.

Discuss the problem of the date of Shakespeare's composition of the Sonnets.

1. No one can say with any certainty exactly when the Sonnets were composed by the author.

2. One thing is fairly certain—they were composed rather early in Shakespeare's career, since Meres mentions their circulation in 1598.

3. Sonnets numbered 138 and 144 were published in corrupt versions in a volume of poetry entitled *The Passionate Pilgrim* (1599). These two sonnets tell us that Shakespeare's friendship was already considerably intimate, and that his love affair with the "dark lady" was also considerably well advanced. They also tell us that Shakespeare's friend and the dark lady had already met; and we are treated to Shakespeare's dark suspicions about his friend's betrayal of their trust. Thus, it is apparent that most of the events depicted in the Sonnets had occurred *before* 1599 at the very latest.

4. Moreover, we know from Shakespeare's early plays that he was very fond of the sonnet form. See, for example *Romeo and Juliet,* published in 1596 (I,v, 96-110), in which play we find that the prologues to the first and second acts are in sonnet form. *Love's Labors Lost* contains at least four sonnets, two in Act I and two in Act V; this play dates as early as 1593. In addition, his early poems (*Venus and Adonis* and *Lucrece*) contain many parallels to the language and ideas of the Sonnets.

5. The years from 1591-1596 enjoyed a popular wave of interest in sonnet writing. Shakespeare no doubt shared in the vogue.

Discuss the use of the words "love" and "lover" in the Sonnets.

In Shakespeare's day the words *love* and *lover* when applied between male friends could and did mean *friendship* and *friend*. The words are used with these meanings in Shakespeare's plays themselves whenever two close male friends are speaking of their friendship for each other, as for example the friends Antonio and Bassanio in the *Merchant of Venice,* or Mercutio and Romeo in *Romeo and Juliet,* to name only a few.

The usage of the day allowed a male friend to sign his letters with the salute of "your lover" as, for example, did John Donne, the poet. Unfortunately, today the words *love* and *lover* between male friends have taken on sexually pejorative meanings which were virtually non-existent in the Renaissance.

What is Shakespeare's attitude toward the "dark lady" referred to so often in Sonnets 127-152?

There is no doubt of Shakespeare's attitude toward the dark lady: it is earthy, unromantic, passionately sexual, often cynical, violently jealous —in short, the very opposite of the usual attitude towards the sonnet heroine so popular in the sonnet sequences of the day. Sonnet 130 describes the dark lady as being the very opposite of the Petrarchan ideal; she was evidently a young, dark-complexioned married woman who, after becoming Shakespeare's acknowledged mistress, turned to his young friend for bedtime comfort. The effect of the betrayal upon Shakespeare is tremendous. In Sonnet 66 he longs for death because he had been "unhappily forsworn." In spite of this, his passionate love for his lady continued ceaselessly to torture him. In the end (Sonnet 146) he seems to have arrived at a feeling of complete revulsion for her:

> For I have sworn thee fair, and thought thee bright,
> Who art as black as hell, as dark as night.

Sonnet 146 is Shakespeare's affirmation of remorse over a love affair for the lady that had begun in emotional exhilaration and had ended in black and cynical despair. This is what makes the Sonnets so unique— these displays of involved emotions are not typical of the sonnet vogue of the day. There is no doubt that the sonnets tell of an actual experience.

Discuss the friendship theme in the Sonnets.

We must remember that Shakespeare was at least a dozen years older than his young friend; we must also keep in mind that the young man was a true aristocrat while Shakespeare was a commoner. Yet the friendship progresses from conventional to genuine love. When they had first met, Shakespeare found the young man unspoiled,, handsome, and charming. What most impressed our poet was his fresh and vibrant youthfulness. The first Sonnets (1-15) urge the young man to marry in order to preserve his beauty and charm in his progeny. For some reason, the young man is reluctant to get married. The theme of the havoc wrought by Time on the preserves of beauty loses its conventional expression in Sonnet 12, where it reaches sublime heights of sadness and regret. When Shakespeare's friend finally met his (Shakespeare's) mistress there was a double betrayal—friend of friend and mistress of lover. Yet, Shakespeare did not hesitate in his decision to stick by his betraying friend, for whom he finds abundant excuses. Moreover, his friendship gave him release from the discontentments of Shakespeare's own existence; it compensated for the discouragements and misfortunes he often encountered in his career; see, for example, the great Sonnet 29 on the compensations of friendship.

Is there disagreement about the historicity of the events reflected in the Sonnets?

There certainly is disagreement ranging all the way from saying that the sonnets are nothing but a fictional expression of a popular and fashionable vogue of the times to declaring that they contain the key with which Shakespeare unlocked he inmost recesses of his heart. Most critics, feel, however, that the sincerity and unconventionality of many of the sonnets indicate a reflection of real experience.

Discuss the evidence indicating that the young man to whom the sonnets are addressed is the Earl of Southampton.

Henry Wriothesley, third Earl of Southampton, was twenty in 1593, a year when most of the sonnets to the youth were written. Shakespeare had dedicated his two erotic poems (*Venus and Adonis* (1593), and *The Rape of Lucrece* (1594) to the Earl, the dedication to *Lucrece* being couched in a language suggesting their close acquaintanceship. Unfortunately, Southampton's initials are H. W. and not "W. H.", whom Thorpe (the publisher of the first edition) calls the "onlie begetter" of the Sonnets. Still, "W. H." is merely H. W. in reverse, and perhaps for some reason Thorpe reversed the initials. Moreover, the Earl was within the Essex circle (the Earl of Essex); and we are well aware of Shakespeare's great admiration for the Earl of Essex as the great hero of England's warriors. For a complete discussion of the infinite ramifications of the theory that the Earl of Southampon was the young man with whom Shakepeare was in love, I suggest that the *Variorum's* exhaustive survey of the progress of the theory be consulted.

Discuss the second most popular candidate for the position of Shakespeare's young man of the Sonnets.

The second most popular candidate for the identity of the youth is William Herbert, the third Earl of Pembroke, an extremely wealthy and generous patron of poets and literature—and a great hater of marriage as an institution (as was the youth of the Sonnets). Both Earls were averse to marriage; both were handsome and stylish youths at the time of the writing of the Sonnets. But if most of the Sonnets were written between 1592-1598 (as seems most probable), there springs up the following difficulty: in 1593 the Earl of Pembroke was only thirteen and Shakespeare twenty-nine, a ridiculous discrepancy. Moreover, for the Earl of Pembroke to be the candidate, style-tests of the Sonnets should support a change in their dating to around 1600 or later. But style-tests of the Sonnets indicate they were indeed written in the early and middle nineties of the sixteenth century. Observe that the Earl of Pembroke's initials are W. H. (William Herbert) and match with the initials of the *"only begetter"* mentioned by the original publisher of the sonnets, Thomas Thorpe. Again, I suggest that the reader consult the *Variorum* (see Bibliography) on the Sonnets for a complete discussion of this fascinating (for those who like puzzles) theory.

Discuss briefly the Petrarchan vogue of sonnet writing.

Petrarch lived from 1304 to 1374 in Italy. At thirteen he saw a girl named Laura who so impressed the sensitive young man that she remained an enduring subject of almost divine inspiration in Petrarch's poems. In 1341 Petrarch was crowned Poet Laureate in Rome for his great learning and humanism. It was he who fixed the form of the sonnet and its various conventions of style and language. The vogue for sonnets dedicated to imaginary or real "Lauras" swept over the continent of Europe and spread eventually to Shakespeare and his contemporaries. Around the 1590's the fad of Petrarchanism in England was already in high gear, with Sir Philip Sidney, Drayton, Daniel, Spenser and others writing whole sequences of love poems to ideal or real women.

Discuss the sonnet as a discipline in form.

The Petrarchan sonnet demands the following:

1. *Discipline.* Within fourteen lines (no more, no less) the poet is to write a poem on a single theme. The development of the theme must follow a rigid form from inception to climax.

2. *Rhyme scheme:* Here discipline is also required, since the pattern of rhymes required immense linguistic resources in like-rhymes. The Petrarchan rhyme scheme used only five different rhymes for fourteen lines. The pattern of rhyming followed this scheme: eight lines rhyming *abba abba* and six lines generally rhyming *cde cde* (or *edc edc* etc.); the last six lines were known as the *sestet,* and the first eight termed the *octave.*

3. The "problem" of the sonnet was stated in the *octave* (or else repeated twice in different metaphors in each of the first two quatrains), and the "solution" to the problem was given in the following *sestet.*

4. The English found the requirements of the Petrarchan form too demanding for their language, which was not so abundant in rhymes as was the Italian. The Elizabethan (or Shakespearean as it is often called) sonnet developed the following rhyme scheme: *abab cdcd efef gg.* The last two rhyming lines are known as the *couplet.* Like the Petrarchan, the statement of the "problem" was put in various forms in the first two *quatrains* (the octave) and "solved" in the remaining *sestet.* All too often the English sonneteer stated the "problem" of the sonnet theme differently in each of the first three quatrains, summing up the solution in a neat aphoristic *couplet—*a decidedly less subtle and complex form than the Italian original. A good many of Shakespeare's sonnets follow this comparatively unsubtle form.

5. The English sonnet used the iambic meter as the underlying rhythm of the sonnet (*iambic* = alternating weak and strong accents), varying the accent here and there to relieve the poem from rhythmic monotony and to add stress to certain words that fell outside the iambic pattern.

6. *In brief:* the form of the Shakespearean sonnet is a poem of fourteen

lines rhyming *abab cdcd efef gg,* the rhythm of which is *iambic penta-meter* (five iambs to a line) and the theme of which is expressed in one of the following ways:

a. The "problem" of the sonnet theme is expressed differently (in metaphor) in each of the first three *quatrains.* The "solution" to the theme is neatly expressed in the concluding *couplet.*

b. The "problem" is stated in the *octave* and the "solution" given in the *sestet.*

c. Some slight variation of the two patterns given above.

Where can I find an analysis in clear terms of the chief Shakespearean sonnets.

The chief and most well-known sonnets are numbers 12, 15, 18, 29, 30, 55, 64, 71, 73, 106, 116, 129 (these are the ones most often discussed and analyzed in college English courses). For a clear and detailed analysis of these sonnets see the above commentaries of those sonnets in this volume under their numbered order. For brief commentaries on the remainder of the 154 sonnets of William Shakespeare, see also above.

BIBLIOGRAPHY

Note: Only the more outstanding works and editions are mentioned here. For an exhaustive bibliography consult H. E. Rollins' *Variorum* edition listed below, or Samuel A. Tannenbaum's *Shakespeare's Sonnets* (*A Concise Bibliography*), New York: Elizabethan Bibliographies, 1940, No. 10. The works are listed chronologically so that critical trends may be traced from their origins:

Richardson, D. L. "On Shakespeare's Sonnets, Their Poetical Merits, and on the Question to Whom They Are Addressed." *The Gentleman's Magazine*, n.s., IV (September, 1835), 250-256; (October, 1835), 361-369.

Simpson, Richard. *An Introduction to the Philosophy of Shakespeare's Sonnets*. London: N. Trübner & Co., 1868.

Dowden, Edward. *Shakspeare: A Critical Study of His Mind and Art*. London: H. S. King & Co., 1875.

Wilde, Oscar. "The Portrait of Mr. W. H." *Blackwood's Magazine*, CXLVI (July, 1889), 1-21. Now in book form, London: Methuen & Co., 1958.

Lee, Sir Sidney. "Shakespeare and the Earl of Southampton." *Cornhill*, LXXVII (April, 1898), 482-495.
——— "Shakespeare and the Earl of Pembroke." *The Fortnightly Review*, LXIX (February 1, 1898), 210-223.

Gollancz Israel, ed. *Shakespeare's Sonnets*. London: J. M. Dent, 1898

Wyndham, George, ed. *The Poems of Shakespeare*. New York: Thomas Y. Crowell, 1898 (?).

Butler, Samuel. *Shakespeare's Sonnets, Reconsidered and in Part Rearranged* . . . London: Longmans, Green and So., 1899.

Lee, Sir Sidney, "Ovid and Shakespeare's Sonnets." *Quarterly Review*, CCX (April, 1909), 455-476.

Shaw, George Bernard. "Preface" to *The Dark Lady of the Sonnets. etc.* London: Constable and Co., Ltd., 1914. Pp. 203-230.

Gray, H. D." "The Arrangement and Date of Shakespeare's Sonnets." *PMLA*, XXX (1915), 629-644.

Alden, Raymond M. "The Poems." *Shakespeare*. New York: Duffield & Co., 1922. Pp. 105-146.

Riding, Laura, and Graves, Robert. "William Shakespeare and E. E. Cummings." *A Survey of Modernist Poetry.* London: William Heinemann, Ltd., 1927. Pp. 49-82.

Chambers, Sir E. K., *William Shakespeare. A Study of Facts and Problems.* 2 vols. Oxford: Clarendon Press, 1930.

Brooke, Tucker. *Shakespeare's Sonnets.* London: Oxford University Press, 1936.

Ransom, John Crowe. "Shakespeare at Sonnets." *Southern Review,* III (January, 1938), 531-553.

Mizener, Arthur. "The Structure of Figurative Language in Shakespeare's Sonnets." *Southern Review,* V (Spring, 1940), 730-747.

Rollins, Hyder Edward. *A New Variorum Edition of Shakespeare: The Sonnets,* 2 vols., Philadelphia: J. B. Lippincott Co., 1944.

Hotson, John Leslie. *Shakespeare's Sonnets Dated and Other Essays.* New York: Oxford University Press, 1949.
——— "When Shakespeare Wrote the Sonnets." *Atlantic Monthly,* CLXXXIV (December, 1949), 61-67.

Baldwin, T. W. *On the Literary Genesis of Shakespeare's Poems and Sonnets.* Urbana: University of Illinois Press, 1950.

Hotson, Leslie. "The Date of Shakespeare's Sonnets." *Times Literary Supplement;* London 2, 1950, p. 348.

Hubler, Edward. *Shakespeare's Songs and Poems.* New York: McGraw Hill Book Co., 1959.

Leishman, J. B. *Themes and Variations in Shakespeare's Sonnets.* New York: Hilary House, 1961.

Craig, Hardin, ed. *The Complete Works of Shakespeare.* Chicago: Scott, Foresman and Company, 1961.

Rowse, A. L. ed. *Shakespeare's Sonnets: Edited with Introduction and Commentary.* New York: Harper & Row, 1964.

Campbell, Oscar J. ed. *The Sonnets, Songs and Poems of Shakespeare.* New York: Bantam Books, 1964.

* chronologically arranged.

MONARCH® *NOTES* AND STUDY GUIDES

ARE AVAILABLE AT RETAIL STORES EVERYWHERE

In the event your local bookseller
cannot provide you with other
Monarch titles you want —

ORDER ON THE FORM BELOW: